E.A. Dustin

Save me Twice

Based on a true story

Save me Twice

Cover photo: Erika Rashka

Published by Verify, LLC

ISBN-13:
978-0692789018 (Save Me Twice) – A WWII story

ISBN-10:
0692789014

Library of Congress Cataloging-in-Publication Data
E.A. Dustin

Save me Twice / by EA Dustin
ISBN-13:
978-0692789018 (Save Me Twice)

ISBN-10:
0692789014

1. World War II- Fiction 2. Concentration Camp Mauthausen – Fiction

---

To Dad
1928 - 2014

Acknowledgements

There are many people to thank for the creation of this book and for helping me tell Karl's story. Thank you all for your patience and time.

Here is a list of those who provided valuable edits, feedback and insights:

Tracey Wong Briggs is a writer/editor; Linda Schaffer is an avid reader and book critic; Eve Pines is a business woman and a critical thinker; Janice Voth is a publications lead and editor; Erika Rashka is a hard working physicist and engineer with many artistic talents; Mary Russo is a medical technician with a keen eye for details; Jean James is retired with loads of wisdom; and Dan Gerber is my co-worker and a hobby historian. Thanks to Lynn Smith for choosing "Save Me Twice" as the book pick for book club and to all the other ladies who personally told me they chose this book for their respective book clubs.

I also appreciate the early feedback and encouragement from Lisa Pettrey-Gill, who is multi-talented; Rose Marie Sanders, who is an avid reader of WWII history; Jackie Dustin, who is hard working, multi-talented, with amazing baking skills; my wonderful supportive siblings; and thanks to Cedric Dustin for the creative input.

Thanks to my Dad Karl who told me his story in verbal and written forms and who patiently answered many of my questions before his passing. Thanks for my Mom for all her patience.

I am truly grateful to each one of you and your inputs. You all live (and have lived) your lives with excellence.

Preface

Propaganda is generally defined as "information, especially of a biased or misleading nature, used to promote or publicize a particular political cause or point of view." (See Wikipedia).

UVA Professor Jerome McGann, during his October 4, 2016 "Thomas Jefferson" award and subsequent timely acceptance speech at UVA, Charlottesville, reminded members of his audience, including me, about Milman Parry's speech: Parry delivered this famous lecture "The Historical Method in Literary Criticism[i]" in 1934, the year before he died, to the Harvard Board of Overseers. The important context of Parry's lecture is signaled by its date, 1934, when "propaganda. . .social changes and confusion" were taking such hold of bewildered people throughout Europe and America. Stalin had assumed control of the Soviets in 1923, Hitler of the Weimar Republic in 1933, and a freewheeling American Capitalism had plunged the United States into a tormented social condition. Parry reflected on that situation during his famous lecture of 1934:

The chief emotional ideas to which men seem to be turning at present. . .are those of nationality—for which they exploit race—and class. . . . Anyone who has followed the history of the use of propaganda for political purposes, with its extraordinary development of intensity and technique in the past fifty years [recognizes how] those who were directing that propaganda expressed their lack of concern, or even contempt, for what actually was so, or actually had been so.[ii]

When Milman Parry gave his lecture then, he couldn't have imagined the magnitude of truth to his words and the incredible horrific impact this propaganda, he warned the Harvard Board of Overseers about, would have in the next decade. Propaganda that exploits race and class helped Hitler become the Fuehrer. Millions fell victim to it. Karl's experience, described in this book, gives a glimpse of the historical consequences. Mainly, we owe it to mankind and it is our responsibility, to not let history repeat itself.[iii]

"Who lives

Who dies

Who tells your story?"[1]

---

[1] Lin-Manuel Miranda "Hamilton" Album

Chapter 1

Arrival

What was that?" Karl jolted up his head from his pillow then tried not to breathe while figuring out the noise. His heart was beating out of his chest. Then he heard it again clearly, another impatient banging at the front door, this one even louder than before. He heard his mother in her slippers hurrying down their squeaky, wooden steps winding toward the front door.

"Who is it?" she asked in a shaky voice. Karl could hear the fear in it. He jumped out from under his warm down comforter, swept aside a strand of red curls off his forehead, and hurriedly tip-toed to his bedroom door to press his ear against it.

"SS. Open the door!" ordered a harsh, deep voice, accompanied by even more impatient banging.

"SS!"

He knew the SS was the German Sturmstaffel, soldiers known for their organized brutality, under Hitler's iron fist. Karl's immediate thoughts went to the Morgenthau family who had recently disappeared. Who were they here for? What were they doing at his family's doorstep this late at night? What could they possibly want? They had been model citizens. These days, nobody dared to be anything else. They stayed pretty much to themselves. Ever since Albert, their Hitler youth leader and former childhood friend, had insisted they attend all Hitler Jugend meetings, they had not missed one.

A scary thought crossed Karl's mind: Is it Mom's radio? They must have caught on to it. He had told her many times to turn that darned thing off. He should have thrown it away. Why else would they be here this late at night? They were forbidden to listen to anything else but the Reichssender, but lately she had tuned in to other, non-German stations, they called the "Feindsender" (enemy station). But she had made sure to keep the volume down so low that nobody from outside could hear it, but Karl knew that they could have traced it. What else could it be?

His mind continued to race. "*Were they bringing news about his missing uncle? Of course not! Not this late in the middle of the night.*" He knew something was very wrong.

He heard the squeaky opening of the heavy oak front door, the small old bell that hung over it chimed with a dull sound.

"Heil, Hitler!" He could hear that there were at least two soldiers, with their heels clicking. He imagined them: in their 30's, armed, tall, and grim, with their arms extended for the Hitler salute.

"Frau Elheusch, wo sind Hans und Karl (Where are Hans and Karl)?" Immediately Karl recognized that voice: Albert! The familiar voice was echoing in their quaint entranceway.

Karl gasped. They were here to get him and his brother. *"Impossible! Why? What difference could they make at this point in October of 1944?"* So many lives had already been lost. Germany was on the retreat from all sides, especially the Eastern front. The German Wehrmacht was running out of recruits at this point. He had heard the call for all boys from age 12 and up to join the war. That's why they were here!

Karl rushed over to his brother Hans's bed only a few feet away; he could barely see, but dim light was seeping through the crack of his bedroom door aiding him in the dark. Mutter had turned on the air raid light bulbs, which during the "darkening law" (Verdunklungs-pflicht) was all that was allowed, in case of an air raid.

Karl shook Hans by the shoulder.

"The SS is here! They are here for us!" Karl frantically tried to wake his brother, but Hans was in a deep sleep. He had been herding cows all day.

"Hmhm," was the only response as Hans rolled back over.

Karl ripped off his white, warm bed cover. "Wake up!" He muffled a frustrated growl, desperate to wake his older brother without making too much noise. At the same time Karl could hear his mother's pleading, high-pitched voice:

"The boys are asleep. What do you want from them? Please Albert, not my boys. They are only kids, not tonight, please come back tomorrow." She started to ramble. Karl couldn't make out all the words, but her cries were getting louder.

"They are children, please don't take them!" Mutter kept begging. Then Karl heard shuffling noises; she was trying to prevent them from going upstairs: following a loud outcry, the hurried footsteps came closer and the heavy boots stopped in front of their bedroom. The door to their room flew open, and at the same time the commanding voice ordered:

"Heil Hitler! Get up!" Karl heard the heels clicking, and then a flashlight powered by a hand generator was pointed at them - it remained lit as long as the soldier squeezed the spring-loaded hand piece. Adjusting to the bright stream of light now glaring into their dark bedroom, squinting, shielding his eyes with his hand, Karl made out the dark silhouettes of two soldiers standing in the door, one much taller than the other, their weapons over their shoulders, powerful, brazen, the arms extended as part of the "Heil, Hitler" sign.

"Heil Hitler!" Karl answered, jumping to extend the Hitler salute, clicking his bare heels together on the cold bedroom floor. Then, in an attempt to calm the situation, he dared to ask, mustering up the most charm possible given the eerie situation: "Hallo Albert, *wie geht's*? (How are you?)

"I am SS-Scharfuehrer Wuest to you!" Albert barked the order. The shadows falling on his face made the frown lines on his forehead appear much deeper than the last time Karl had seen him.

"Get dressed!" demanded the shorter SS soldier, pacing swiftly. Karl didn't recognize this sandy-brown haired soldier. "We have orders. You are to come with us! You are joining the SS; you will serve your Vaterland! Heil, Hitler!"

"Why tonight? Can't you come back in the morning?" Mutter cried in vain from behind the men.

"Wake him up!" Albert demanded, his head gesturing toward Hans.

"Mmmm." Hans was making an inaudible sound.

"Hans wake up!" Karl grabbed Hans' shoulder again.

Hans slowly sat up, looking dazed, and trying to make sense of the ruckus.

"What?" he asked. As he awoke he noticed the red SS patch on the soldiers' arms, reflecting in the light. He quickly realized: SS soldiers were there in his house. Why? He scooted his body back toward the headboard, away from the glaring light.

"What should we pack?" he heard Karl inquiring.

"Where are we going?" Hans asked incredulously.

Instead of responding, Albert went on to demand, "Where is Hermann?"

Karl responded, in near shock, "Why do you need Hermann? He can't do anything for you or to serve the Vaterland. You know he is in a wheelchair. Why don't you leave him be?"

"We have orders to take him, too. We have to take him to a home," Albert coldly responded, looking down.

"A home? He doesn't need to be in a home. He is fine here!" Karl responded, getting more scared now for his handicapped brother than for himself.

Albert walked toward the next bedroom and opened the door, looking for Hermann. He knew this house inside out; he had spent much time here just a few years back. He found Hermann in his bed awakened by the ruckus; Hermann had always been a light sleeper. He squinted, adjusting to the flashlight being pointed at him.

"Hermann, get dressed," Albert demanded. "You are coming with us."

Albert looked at the other SS: "Gefreiter Ferdinand, once Hermann is dressed, let's carry him downstairs, put him in his wheelchair!"

The other SS Ferdinand hesitated, seeming puzzled. With a lowered voice, he leaned in toward Albert. "Albert, really, do we, do we really need to take the handicapped boy? We are here for the healthy ones to help join the war. Why take the cripple?"

Hermann's head was down as the commotion was happening around him. He looked defeated and helpless.

"Yes, don't take him. Don't!" Both Hans and Karl were pleading.

"We know what Hitler thinks about the handicapped!"

"Please don't take Hermann. Please! Albert, you played soccer with us. Hermann was our goalie, and a good one. He is your neighbor. Who knows what will happen to him in a home? Please don't. Please!" Karl now stretched out his arms in front of Hermann, trying to shield him.

Albert then angrily ripped the Karabiner 43 rifle off his shoulder and quickly aimed it at them; the frown lines above his dark-brown eyes had narrowed. "You two get dressed *sofort* (quickly) or else!" Turning to Ferdinand, Albert hissed, "We have orders. You know what Hitler thinks about this kind of waste of a person!"

Hans and Karl yanked up their hands. They both turned pale. How dare Albert threaten them and talk like that about their brother! With the rifle pointed at them, though, there wasn't much they could do. What would happen to their brother?

Ferdinand reluctantly turned away from Albert, and as if just remembering that he was the lower ranked SS officer, he dejectedly agreed: "Heil Hitler, *Dein Wort ist mein Befehl* (Your word is my order)."

Both Hans and Karl took a few steps backwards and with Albert's rifle still aimed at them, they held up their hands. They backed away until they hit the wall on the other side of Hermann's room, not once losing eye contact with the SS. Albert slowly lowered his weapon down by his side. "This is no joke!"

Hans and Karl lightly exhaled. Albert had always been a sore loser with a scary hair-trigger temper. It was curtailed once more.

"Don't worry about packing anything besides your Hitler Jugend uniform, bring some underwear and socks, and the Wehrmacht will provide the rest. Hurry! We don't have all night! Schnell! Schnell!" Albert now rushed them along.

As fast as they could move, Karl and Hans opened the top drawer of their shared dresser, pulling out sweaters. "No, you don't need that!" The shorter SS soldier, Ferdinand, slammed the drawer shut. "Only your Hitler Jugend uniforms!"

The boys instead grabbed for their freshly pressed Hitler Jugend uniforms in the middle drawer. They also got the dark blue woolen caps with the visor and a Hitler Youth pin on the front. The sides of the cap buckled in front in the up position and could be pulled down over the ears. They also grabbed their dark blue wool trousers and the matching three-button pullovers, their black polished shoes and their Hitler Youth arm patches.

"You won't need the patches!" Ferdinand commanded again.

They then dressed as fast as they could under the watch of the two soldiers.

Mutter tried to intervene again. "Mutter, stop, it's useless!" Hans walked up to her outside Hermann's room and tried to calm her.

"Frau Elheusch, *nein,* stay out! This is Fuehrer business; you are not to get involved!" Ferdinand said. "Your sons will be serving the Fuehrer – it's the best for the Vaterland. You should be very proud of them! And Hermann will be in good hands!" Hans seemed to see a slight sadness crossing Ferdinand's face.

"Nooooooo!" she shrieked. The sound reminded Karl of the screeching pigs he had heard at his butcher shop often right before they got slaughtered.

"Mutter, we'll be alright," he intended to sooth, unconvincingly. He was now dressed and tried to console her, hugging her tightly.

Karl whispered as softly as he could to calm her, while holding her tight: "It's alright, Mutter. We are fine, we will be fine, I promise you, Hermann will be fine. They are armed. There is nothing we can do. Please control yourself, Mutter. It will all be all right, if we just do what they say!"

Hans joined Mutter and Karl in their embrace, leaning in and wrapping his arms around both of them. "Karl is right. Hermann will be fine. Don't cry! We'll be back before you know it. You have to stay strong for us. You have to keep the store running. You have to help Opa get the desk finished. It's so close to being done." It took all his inner strength to get these words out while holding back tears.

"Enough of that. *Schnell!* Let's go. We don't have much time!" Impatiently Albert grabbed Hans's arm away from his mother. With his other hand, he also grabbed Karl's sleeve and yanked him ahead of both of them.

“Alright, alright, we are going. You don’t have to push us,” Karl pulled away his arm from Albert, and straightened out his sleeves, as they were rushed down the steps.

“Stay down here, we will get Hermann,” Albert ordered and marched back upstairs to Hermann’s room. “Get dressed, Hermann. We are taking you to a home!”

“No! I am not going to a home!” Hermann responded, defiantly.

“Please don’t take him. He is fine here. He can’t help your war. He is no use to you. Please, please, not Hermann, too,” pleaded Mutter again, who repeatedly tried to enter the room, with Ferdinand covering the doorway.

“Frau Elheusch, enough of that! Hermann is coming with us. Those are orders! Help Hermann get dressed or step aside!” Albert demanded.

“Mutter, let it be.” Hans and Karl had come back up to support Hermann, but now really worried for her safety, knowing armed Albert’s unpredictable temper, Hans grabbed Mutter by the shoulder and gently guided her to the side.

“I can help!” Karl offered. With his hands up, he cautiously stepped into Hermann’s room, to not startle the two soldiers while carefully gauging their reaction. They reluctantly allowed Karl to help with his brother, something he did every day: Karl helped Hermann sit up while Mutter now also eagerly jumped in to get Hermann’s clothes. Everyone then somberly and quietly dressed him, with Hermann doing his part to help. Only their mother’s sniffles could be heard.

After Hermann was dressed, Karl and Hans grabbed him under his knees to lift him up in a well-practiced routine, and then carried him downstairs.

“Take that wheelchair, Albert!” Karl ordered the SS, pointing to it sitting beside the stairwell. Albert had helped with the wheelchair many times before, when they still were playmates.

The SS soldier unfolded the rusty wheelchair and rolled it to the bottom of the staircase so the two brothers could place Hermann into it.

“Let me grab your coat, Hermann,” Mutter rushed to the coat closet to grab his winter coat and a hand-knit black scarf. She hastily put it on Hermann and then lovingly wrapped the scarf around his neck. She buttoned up his coat, tucked in his scarf, while her eyes again filled with tears. “You take good care of yourself.” She kissed his forehead then hugged Hermann tightly. Hans and Karl looked on helplessly.

Hermann also knew what Hitler thought about the handicapped: that they were a burden to society and didn’t deserve to live. At this point he was very scared. He started to shiver.

“Enough of that, we need to go!” Albert demanded impatiently. “Hans and Karl, you are coming with me. Ferdinand will take Hermann to the home. “

The soldier opened the front door, pushed Hans and Karl in front of him, with Ferdinand wheeling Hermann behind them. Then both of the soldiers stopped to click their heels one last time, stretched out their arms to salute, and said “Heil Hitler” in unison to Mutter, in a fleeting moment of respect to her. She helplessly stood there and watched them take her three sons that night, not knowing whether she would ever see them again.

****

Her Blackberry displays 2:50 pm. Her dad's plane was supposed to have landed five minutes ago. Rushing into the airport, she takes comfort in knowing that it will take him 20 minutes or more to get through customs, even if the flight arrived on time. "*Phew!*" she says to herself as she takes a deep breath and blows away a strand of pesky bangs. She is sweating in her heavy winter coat and rips it off to carry it in her arms. She exhales slowly. Glancing at a reflection of her slender silhouette in an airport shop window, she doesn't approve of what's looking back at her. It has been rainy and windy outside and she is disheveled, clothes and hair damp and unruly, a frizzy mess. She comforts herself with the thought that her dad will just be happy to see her. With her right hand, she crunches her hair into some manageable curls.

Moving on, she checks one of the many "Arrivals" monitors. The status of flight 4598 from Frankfurt to Dulles International Airport flashes the "landed" sign.

"Good," she is relieved, "He got here safely!" She slows down to a leisurely walk. She always worries about these overseas flights, even though she knows that flying is supposedly one of the safest ways to travel. As she follows the international arrival signs, her heels clicking on the cold airport floor, she questions how these safety statistics are gathered. "*When they compare the safety of the different ways to travel, are they realistically comparing the same amount of people traveling by car, train, and motorcycle given the same amount of time? Maybe those statistics are just looking at distance traveled, and sure, a plane can cover more distance and carry more people at the same time*," she thinks, continuing her analysis of this puzzling travel statistic.

Ellie finally arrives at the international arrival gate: Guard rails block off a square area around the large, steel, double-doors through which all the international passengers are expected to walk. She has been here at this spot many times, to pick up friends returning from overseas trips or relatives coming to visit. So she is not surprised to see the crowd of people that has already gathered.

She joins the crowd standing along the guardrails. She notices some people appear anxious. Some of them probably haven't seen their loved ones or friends in years, and some are excited to see their relatives after weeks or days. Limousine and taxi drivers are standing off to the side, holding up signs with names of people they are paid to pick up.

Standing there waiting for her Dad she wonders how he feels about coming to the US. This first trip to the U.S. must have such special meaning to him. Her thoughts drift temporarily to her dad's life in Germany and his stories about WWII. How scared he must have been the night the SS snatched him and his brothers from his Mother's house nearly 60 years ago.

“Excuse me!” Someone’s trying to get in front of Ellie to get a better view of whose arriving at the airport. What a tragic night for her Dad, uncles and grandma that had been. She now again scans the crowd.

A little boy about 4 years old is holding a red balloon in one hand and in his other he is holding a young woman’s hand. The woman is wearing a beautiful grey woolen suit with immaculately placed black buttons. “*I wonder where she bought that suit*,” Ellie sighed, knowing she probably wouldn’t be able to afford it. It is perfectly tailored and the material looks exquisite.

Ellie notices an elderly woman standing there with a bouquet of tulips in her hands. It’s springtime in DC, and tulips can be seen everywhere in yards, gardens, stores, and restaurants.

What a great idea. “Tulips to welcome Papa would be nice,” Ellie decides, and she walks over to the nearby flower vendor and picks out a bouquet of red tulips.

“Ten dollar,” the vendor says in his heavy Korean accent, holding out his hand.

Ellie hands him a $10 bill. “*Airport prices*!” Ellie sighs to herself as she walks back, trying to claim her spot in the crowd, which is getting larger by the minute.

Her dad had always kept a tulip garden at her childhood home in Germany. Red tulips were his favorite, even though he grew them in almost any color imaginable, even multicolored. Though he had to give up gardening years ago, as it had become too hard on his aging knees. "*He will be happy to see these*," Ellie thought, admiring her bouquet.

"*I wonder how he is feeling after this long flight. How is his heart holding up*?" She worries again. How did she let five years pass by without seeing him? She had visited Germany for two weeks back then, and now he had put himself through the ordeal of this long overseas flight. How fast the time has passed by! She shakes her head quietly. He has been having heart problems. Thirty-five years ago, he had his first heart attack at age 40. The doctor had warned him to stop smoking or else. He had instantly stopped his habit of smoking two-packs of HBs a day. She remembers the cigarette brand, as she often had to fetch a package for him at the cigarette machine installed in front of her uncle's house across the street. Ellie was just a kid then, but now questions herself as an enabler because of always getting the cigarettes for him. The heart attack really had scared him, and he realized surviving it was another chance at life. He has been having heart issues since.

For the past 10 years, they have called each other almost every weekend: She has convinced him to buy a computer and taught him how to use the barely known then free phone service Skype, so they could avoid those large overseas phone bills of the past. They also stay in touch writing letters, though she used to write many more.

Ellie initially came to the DC area during a summer to take a few college courses at one of the local universities. She fell in love with the hard working people, inventive attitudes and the bustling culture, along with the museums, sports games and the surrounding lakes and hiking paths appealed to her love of the outdoors. The DC area offerings were so much broader than her village upbringing. A company eventually sponsored her work visa and supported her through all the immigration and visa paperwork. In 1995 she became a US citizen and has been living in Northern Virginia all of her adult life.

She is in deep thought as the door swings open and the first passenger steps through: a tall blond handsome man in his thirties, pushing his large matching suitcases. "Dad!" Ellie hears the little balloon-boy's high pitched scream and he loosens the grip from the woman in the woolen grey suit and darts toward the man with open arms. "Dad!" the boy screams again and flies into the arms of his dad, who is now crouched down to scoop up his little boy.

Ellie wonders how long the boy's dad had been gone. Has he been on a business trip? Did he visit family? Did he immigrate after them? The little family looks so happy to see each other again.

The doors swing open again, and a slew of teenagers dressed in matching soccer uniforms, energetically joking and laughing with each other, showing their colorful braces, is bouncing through. When Ellie was that age she was the only one in her class with braces; nowadays, they are a fashion statement and every teenager seems to have them. A few middle-aged women who have been expressively chatting with each other now turn toward the teens, followed by a noisy welcome with energetic hugging and laughing.

The woman in the grey suit follows her husband with his son beaming tight in his arms and she now hands their luggage to a driver. They are now disappearing in the crowd.

Ellie looks away from the spectacles, and an elderly man emerges through the door. She recognizes her dad, Karl. How quickly he got through customs! Ellie is pleasantly surprised.

Overjoyed she runs toward him with open arms: “Papa!” she screams. For a second she feels as thrilled as that little boy with the red balloon. For a second she is a little kid again.

He immediately picks her out from the crowd and his wrinkled face turns into an enormous smile. Stopping his cart loaded with two large brown suitcases, he waits for her with open arms. They squeeze each other tightly, almost crushing the tulips. She quickly remembers and hands them to him, as one of the tulip pedals falls onto the cold airport floor, tears of happiness collecting in her eyes.

“Oh, red tulips!” he says, as he admires them. Then he looks at her. “You haven’t changed a bit!”

Ellie studies him, glancing at him sideways. “Your teeth look different!”

He laughs. His middle daughter never missed the slightest change. Even as a kid, she noticed even his touch-up haircuts or his slightest change in facial expressions, always able to gauge his moods; and there definitely had been a cadre of mood swings given his undiagnosed PTSD from the war. Being raised by a Hitler Youth educated father had not always been easy for her.

"Yes," he says, "I had two dental implants put in here in the front" — he points to his top front teeth. Forgetting for a minute that he is feeling weak, Karl is beaming, happy to see his daughter after all these years. He continues to evaluate her. She looks happy, so grown up and sophisticated in her matching white blouse and black skirt with black pumps. Her soft childlike features have sharpened.

Papa has aged. Ellie continues to assess him: He is 75 now, but to her he looks even older. He looks pale and weak!

A Jewish man, distinguished by his Kippah, walks by. Karl flinches ever so slightly, as if he wants to duck and hide in shame. Ellie notices. His time in World War II, even only at 16, stays with him, no matter how much time has passed. Ellie ignores his reaction.

"How was the flight?" she asks.

"The food was ok. You know I am very picky," he smirks. Ellie laughs: he hasn't changed, she knows too well the food connoisseur her dad is. Only the food grown from his own garden and generally his own cooking were the best.

"Hopefully it wasn't too fatty?" she continues, as always concerned for this health.

A shadow seems to fall over his face. His heart had been bothering him during the flight, his pulse at times was too low for him to detect, and he had chest pains. He doesn't want to worry her. He is now out of breath pushing the suitcases.

"Here let me get that," she says as she grabs the handles from him to push the cart. She takes over without any complaints from him.

"What's the matter, Dad?" she asks, concerned.

“Ah nothing much, you know, my old heart,” he pauses and hesitates to say more.

“Are you in pain?” she worries

“No, just my heart… the usual,” he brushes off her concerns, while trying to catch his breath.

“Dad, what is it? Just tell me what’s wrong!” she demands, getting impatient.

“Well, my heart. It’s been bothering me during this flight.”

“Ok, I am dialing 911!”

“Nope!” he grabs for Ellie’s blackberry. “Don’t! I am fine!”

“No, you need to go to the hospital!”

“No, it’s ok! This is not new, it all started at home,” he says slowly with a lowered voice and now labored breathing, “I picked up a prescription on Friday. So it’s only been a few days since I started taking this new medication. Maybe it’s just now kicking in, having this strange effect. Also, the flight seems to have worsened things. You know the air in those cabins is so thin, sometimes I feel I can’t breathe up there.”

Ellie is now really concerned “Ok, let’s sit down over here at this coffee shop. Let me feel your pulse.” She hooks her right arm under his and struggles with her left hand to push his cart filled with the heavy suitcases to the nearest empty table at the coffee shop. She then grabs her Dad’s hand to help him sit down. She wraps her two fingers and thumb around his wrist to feel his pulse and compares it to the seconds ticking along on her Blackberry timer. “Dad, your pulse does seem slow!” she now feels really alarmed.

"You probably shouldn't have taken this long overseas flight then. I warned you about that. I was worried about your heart. You just now got new heart medication, too?! Did your doctor even say it's OK for you to fly? Remember, we talked about you getting her approval." Ellie feels annoyed and at the same time frantic.

"Since when do I need to ask a doctor whether I can come see my daughter?" he laughs weakly in an attempt to joke. "But yes, I told Dr. Magdalene that I am coming to see you, and she didn't say I couldn't." Dr. Magdalene was their small town family doctor who treated him since his first heart attack. She also treated Ellie when she was a child.

"*Typical*!" she thinks, defeated. Her dad is being his stubborn self.

"Dad you don't look too good." she says. "Let me at least call a doctor."

"Let's just sit here a bit longer. I just need to take a break." Karl says accompanied by labored breathing. "I'll be fine," he tries to reassure her slouched in the uncomfortable coffee shop chairs. "Please get me a glass of water. That always makes me feel better."

"Papa, I can get you water, but I think you need an ambulance?" Ellie insists.

Karl refuses "Don't exaggerate, Ellie. I don't need an ambulance. Just let me sit here for a bit, I'll be fine in just a minute. The flight was just exhausting for your old father."

Ellie studies him, calming down a bit. He might be right; he might just need to rest a bit. She orders a glass of water without ice at the counter and brings it over. "Here, drink this all up."

Watching him gulp the water, she suggests, “Papa, maybe I can get you a wheelchair to get you out of this airport,” and immediately she gets up and says, “You stay right here. I’ll get you a wheelchair so I can wheel you to my car, and then I want to bring you to one of the best cardiologists in the area. I’ll find you one here in Georgetown. Only the best doctor for you,” Ellie insists.

“No,” Karl refuses “I don’t need to see a doctor. Bring me to your house, I just need to rest; I’ll be fine.”

“Dad, this is not the time to be stubborn!” Ellie disagrees.

~~~~
~~~~

Chapter 2

The Doctor's Visit

Dr. Schlesinger's graduate degree and her other medical accomplishments are lined up perfectly in dark brown wooden frames, covering almost every inch of her white office walls.

The blood pressure cuffs are tightly gripping Karl's upper arm. Exhausted, he is slouched sideways in the uncomfortable wooden chair in the Georgetown doctor's small office.

"90 over 48," says the nurse.

Ellie translates for him *"neunzig ueber achtundvierzig,"* and her dad knows that this is low, especially in light of his high blood pressure.

"I'll get a glass of water," Dr. Schlesinger's assistant, Michelle, offers.

Ellie had called Dr. Schlesinger's number from the airport. Her co-worker Janice had been praising the cardiologist for months, ever since Janice's mom had heart bypass surgery. Within weeks her mother was almost back to her normal self, and Janice credited Dr. Schlesinger's outstanding expertise. Ellie had always thought in the back of her mind that her dad could benefit from seeing this doctor. She wondered how she could get him to come here, given he was a world away, but never brought it up because she knew he would not travel this far to see a cardiologist. Now here he was, sitting in her office much sooner than Ellie could have anticipated.

An airport porter had ended up helping her with pushing the cart full of suitcases, while she got that wheelchair for her dad, who then had reluctantly climbed into it.

Once in her car, she had Googled "Georgetown cardiologists Dr. Schlesinger" on her Blackberry and Dr. Schlesinger, cardiologist in

Georgetown quickly came up in the search with impressive credentials: medical degree from Cornell University; internship at Johns Hopkins; specializes in coronary artery disease, and the list of credentials went on and on. Ellie had called the number listed.
An older sounding woman answered: “Dr. Schlesinger’s office, Michelle speaking.”
“I need to make an appointment today for my dad.”
“Sorry, we are completely booked today; if you are having a medical emergency you need to call 911.”
Ellie had pleaded, “My dad has just arrived at Dulles airport from an overseas flight from Germany. He is having hard time breathing.”
“In that case you should call 911!” Michelle reiterated.
“No,” Ellie insisted “he just needs to be seen by an American cardiologist. He is already under cardiology care in Germany, but we want to get a second opinion. I specifically picked Dr. Schlesinger because of her reputation. I want to be sure my dad is seen by one of the best cardiologists I can find in the area. Please!?”
Then there was a long pause that ended in a deep sigh and the assistant Michelle gave in “All right, OK, then, I can try to squeeze you in if you are here within the hour.”
“We’ll be there!” Ellie confirmed, even though she suspected given the area traffic it would take her more than an hour to get there.

After entering the address into the Blackberry’s GPS, Ellie drove her dad straight from the airport to Dr. Schlesinger’s office, despite her dad’s attempts at resistance. “You know I just need a good night’s rest," he had protested, but Ellie was determined. She didn't want to risk her dad being wrong about his self-diagnosis and ignored his incessant complaints about not wanting to go to see "this American doctor."

In her mind, Ellie is cursing the socialized health care in Germany, where, in her experience, younger patients' health care takes priority over anyone's who is over 60. Take a 40-year- old father of three kids versus a 75-year-old man whose kids are grown: In the socialized health care system, the 40-year-old's health will take priority. In Germany, a socialist country, her dad's health had already been put on the "back burner."

Dr. Schlesinger is in her late 30s with shoulder length brown locks elegantly framing her face. Ellie translates during the entire visit with Dr. Schlesinger; her dad speaks only a few words of English, and Dr. Schlesinger doesn't speak any German.

After introducing herself and her dad, Ellie quickly fills in the doctor: This is hardly how he had envisioned this trip at all. Here he was a continent away from home, in Washington, DC, with plans to visit his daughter for only a few weeks, and his first day is spent in a cardiologist's office.

Ellie translates. "He thinks his new medication is causing the issue. His doctor prescribed it recently."

"Does he have it with him?" Dr. Schlesinger asks.

Yes he had brought it, because they knew the doctor would want to see it. Her Dad pulls out a plastic sandwich bag with various colors of medication containers in it. "Sure it's right here." He pulls out a brown bottle and hands it to Dr. Schlesinger. She inspects the name typed on the side of it. “I am familiar with this medication. We will need to do a thorough check-up first, before I can tell whether the medication could be causing the problem. Please tell your dad that we’ll do an EKG now and we’ll continue to monitor his blood pressure during the EKG. You can wait here.”

Ellie continues to translate for her dad so he knows what to expect next, and then one of the assistants wheels Karl to the room next door.

“Please come and get me if you need anything translated,” Ellie calls after the assistant.

Ellie then sits down in a nearby chair, feeling anxious. She picks up the blinking Blackberry sticking out of her purse and clicks to read her new work email message; but its content is not registering; her mind is with her dad. ”*What if he is seriously sick? Can this doctor help him? Would he have to go to a hospital here? How would she get him back to Germany? She would have to call his travel insurance and see what they cover. If he needs surgery, it might be best for him to get back to Germany to be around all his relatives and friends. What if she needs to get him on the earliest flight back? Would the airlines even let him back on a flight? Will the doctor there in Germany be able to help him?*” The worried thoughts are coming non-stop.

She decides to type an email to her siblings in Germany. They are six hours ahead, and it would be close to 10:30 pm. She doesn’t expect them to read it until the morning, except her oldest sister, perhaps, whom she knows has sleep problems and spends time on the computer whenever she can't sleep. She tells them in the email that Dad has arrived safely and that they are now at a cardiologist's office in Georgetown, but not to worry. She will keep them all posted when they are done with the cardiologist, and she will send a follow-up email.

After 15 minutes, which seems more like an hour to Ellie, Dr. Schlesinger calls her into the check-up room where her dad is laying on the exam table, covered in a gown.

"The EKG shows some irregularities. I want to give him a heart echocardiogram to get an even more detailed picture, if that's okay with him. Can you ask him to give his approval?"

Ellie translates, telling her dad it's only for the best, and at this point, he approves quickly. Dr. Schlesinger seems to be making him feel comfortable. There is something trustworthy about her demeanor.

The assistant rolls in the heart echocardiogram machine and she hooks Karl up to it, while Ellie is watching from only a few feet away. Ellie notices he has put on a few pounds and many more rolls of fat are layering his stomach than the last time she had seen her Dad working shirtless in his garden. It makes Ellie feel a bit uncomfortable to see her Dad that out of shape, especially since she remembers him as very muscular man even until right when she left for the U.S.

"Dad, should I wait outside?" she asks, not wanting to intrude on his privacy.

"No, no, please stay," he insists. "I need you to translate. Also, I don't want to be alone in here."

To quiet her mind while the test is being conducted, Ellie distracts herself by reading the additional framed credentials on the wall. Dr. Schlesinger waves her to come closer. "I'd like to show you something. Please translate for your dad. Pull up closer." Dr. Schlesinger points to the empty chair sitting at the end of the room.

Pulling up the chair to the desk, Ellie tries to focus on the heart echo-cardiogram screen display Dr. Schlesinger is pointing to, with a gray mass displayed on the monitor. With both Karl and Ellie looking on, Dr. Schlesinger motions to an area of the screen:

"Here the blood flow is very good; you can see the regular heartbeat, resulting in high blood flow," she describes the area where the heart is pulsating regularly and the mass is full, then continuing her pointing motions she moves to the outer edge of the heart, to the area that's flatter than the rest of the mass: "See this? This is what's called an enlarged area of the heart, and here hardly any blood is flowing through. You can barely see the heart pulsating here. The area here is much flatter, and it appears somehow his heart has been damaged in this area." Ellie can see the difference from the mass of the pulsating heart area to the thinner outlying area.

"Also," Dr. Schlesinger continues "a healthy heart size ends around here," while motioning to the edge of three-quarters of the heart. "Your dad's heart is enlarged."

Ellie's started to feel nauseated looking at her dad's heart on a monitor, while having to listen to all the problems with it. She doesn't really understand the significance of each problem. Can they be fixed? She has so many questions, but before asking, Ellie slowly turns to her dad, who has been watching and hearing the discussion, looking worried and puzzled and at the same time resigned. Ellie translates, repeating the same pointing motions on the monitor from Dr. Schlesinger and explains what she was told.

Dr. Schlesinger continues her diagnosis, "It could be that your dad had a cold or some type of viral infection, and this enlargement is the by-product of it. Or," she hesitates "it could be from too much alcohol. Did your dad drink a lot when he was younger, or is he still a heavy drinker now?"

"No," Ellie assures the doctor without asking her dad, "Drinking is not an issue now." When her Dad was much younger, before he was even married to her mother, in his single days he had his share of beer and schnapps and drunken episodes, but drinking hasn't been and isn't an issue since he got married. Her sisters would have told her if that had changed. She would know.

"It must be caused by an infection, the flu perhaps or a cold." Ellie insists.

She knows her dad well enough. Ellie reluctantly translates the question including her immediate answer to her dad, and he confirms, "No, I really don't drink much at all, a glass of wine here or there, but that's it." And then he adds, looking for reassurance: "A glass of red wine here and there is supposed to be even healthy, isn't it?"

"What does this mean? Does he need surgery, heart bypass surgery or what do you think needs to be done for him? What is needed for an enlarged heart?" Ellie's turns to Dr. Schlesinger, and now her questions just pour out, as she is not trying to conceal her worry any longer. Seeing a portion of her dad's heart, displayed on that monitor, that doesn't have much blood flow to it is very disconcerting. "Is this a common heart problem?" Her anxiety is now obvious to everyone in the room.

Dr. Schlesinger tilts her head and says "He needs a stent to his heart. That will support the artery leading to the unhealthy portion. I also have to put him on different blood thinners. I need to adjust his medication, and should be good as new." She smiled in a warm, calming manner. "The medication he is on right now is absolutely the wrong kind: I would never prescribe that type of medication for your dad's current condition. The medication they prescribed slows down the heartbeat even further. This might have been useful for some of his other heart issues in the past, but I suggest he stops taking it. Since I am not his doctor and don't have his entire heart history, I could put him on a really mild version of the type of medication I think he needs, and if you all approve, I will write a prescription now. I recommend we keep him in the hospital overnight to monitor how he reacts to the new prescription. I can put the stent in within a week. But that will require hospital stay, and I am not sure his insurance will cover it."

Karl wants to know what's going on: *"Was sagt sie?"* ("What is she saying?") Ellie translates. As she translates, Ellie starts to feel angry at her dad's house doctor, Dr. Magdalena. How could she prescribe the wrong medication? When was the last time she checked his dad's heart thoroughly? Did she ever even do a heart echocardiogram, or did she simply prescribe the same medication or different variations of it, which the doctor had given his dad over the last 20 or so years. Ellie doubts Dr. Magdalena, from their small village, would even have the heart echocardiogram equipment in her small town family practice. But even if she didn't have it, Dr. Magdalena could have referred her Dad to a doctor in the city who had the equipment.

Ellie knew her Dad's answer before she even finished translating. "No Ellie, I will not have surgery here in the U.S. – no way, completely out of the question!"

Ellie informs Dr. Schlesinger of her dad's decision.

"I recommend then that he fly back home as soon as possible to see his doctor, but it will be on his own risk. Your dad needs to have that surgery as soon as possible, and with this specific dose I am giving him, he needs to be monitored closely until we are sure it's the right dose. I will write-up a report and recommendations that your dad can give to his doctors to follow up."

"Sounds good! Is it safe to bring my dad back to my house overnight, until we can get him a flight back?"

Dr. Schlesinger shakes her head vehemently. "Sorry, no. Like I said, I highly recommend he spend the night at the hospital and is monitored. We can't exactly predict his reaction to this medication. At least in the hospital, if his condition worsens, someone will be right there to help."

Right, Dr. Schlesinger did recommend that earlier. Ellie is too stressed to think clearly. Having her dad spend the night at the hospital is sound advice, and Ellie agrees.

Dr. Schlesinger then writes up the instructions for her dad to take back home to Dr. Magdalena, and she would have to follow those closely.

“You are going to the hospital for at least one night!” Ellie orders her Dad. She is not really asking his permission, because she knows he would try to resist.

“Also I’ll get you on a flight back as quickly as possible. I will also call your insurance. And please, don’t see Dr. Magdalena when you go back. Please go straight to the hospital in Nuernberg. They will have better facilities and better equipment, and the doctors there will have the most recent up to date education, just like Dr. Schlesinger here.” Ellie also informs Karl that Dr. Schlesinger thinks that Dr. Magdalena prescribed the wrong type of medication.

“Dad – has Dr. Magdalena ever run a heart echocardiogram on you using a similar machine to this one here?”

As Ellie suspected, her dad answers no, he has never seen such state-of-the-art equipment.

A knock on the door interrupts the intimate check-up and discussions, and the office assistant sticks her head half-in, as if too embarrassed to walk in: “I am sorry, Ms. Elheusch, but we can’t accept the German health insurance you provided us.”

Ellie is not too surprised, “Ok, can I write a check? When my Dad is back in Germany he can file the claim with his insurance then. He has international health insurance.”
Dr. Schlesinger responds to the assistant, “Don’t charge them for the heart echocardiogram that would be $1,500 by itself. Only bill them for the EKG and the general office visit.”
Ellie is now taken aback by the unexpected kindness. Never has she met a doctor that generous; she actually had expected a high bill from this visit.
Ellie translates for her dad, who now is aghast by Dr. Schlesinger’s generosity. “Not sure we can accept that, Ellie!” His pride is now showing through.
“It’s ok, Dad, if she doesn’t want to bill us for it, just accept it gracefully!”
Karl turns to Dr. Schlesinger sticking out his hand, “Sank you, Sank you,” one of the few English expressions he actually is able to repeat in his heavy German accent.
Dr. Schlesinger responds, “Oh don’t worry about it at all, do you know my dad is originally from Southern Germany. He came here in 1946.”
“Yes, Schlesinger is a very common German last name.” Ellie says.
“No, that’s actually my married name. My husband also has German ancestry – I am surrounded by Germans.” She attempts a tired smile.
On any other day, Ellie would have asked Dr. Schlesinger more about her Dad, where in Germany he is from, how he came here, etc., but they are running out of time. Ellie is always interested in

folks with German ancestry and has heard from so many Americans about their German ancestors. She isn't too surprised that the doctor with the German last name was one of them. But her dad finds the story fascinating: "Ask her where her dad is from in Southern Germany or knows whether any of her relatives still live in Germany?" He seems to be getting his energy back now that he knows the adjusted medication should make him feel better.

But Dr. Schlesinger quickly instructs the assistant "Mary, call an ambulance and make all the necessary arrangements. Let's send him to Fairfax Hospital for the night, so he can be monitored there."

Ellie tells her dad about the plans. He is trying a weak attempt at protesting, but realizes this decision has been made. After what seems forever, the ambulance arrives. Ellie is allowed to sit in the back with her dad while he is transported to the hospital.

Once he is checked in at the hospital and resting comfortably, Ellie decides to stay the night in the room with him.

"No, Ellie, you go home and get a good night's rest. I am fine here; I am in good hands."

She insists she will stay. Before too long, the long overseas trip is catching up with him, and he falls into a deep slumber.

Chapter 3

Background

Karl was six years old when Hitler became Fuehrer (Leader) of Germany in 1934. Four years later, when Karl turned 10, his school required he become a member of an organization called the German Young People (Deutsche Jugend DJ). At 14, he was required to join the Hitler Jugend (Hitler Youth). As all boys aged 14 to 18 years old, he and his brother, Hans, didn't have any choice other than to join and attend.

The three brothers Karl, Hans, Hermann, lived with their Mutter (mom) in their Opa's (grandpa's) house in a small village, nestled in the hills and valleys at the outskirts of Nuremberg (Nuernberg). Red, curly-haired, and green eyed, Karl was the youngest and fairest of the three teenagers, each two years apart. His older brother Hans' hair was blonder with blue eyes and his skin was redder. Hermann, the oldest at 19, had red hair with freckles covering his forehead and nose. Hermann had to use a wheelchair to get around. Hermann kept his hair long. It was his way to rebel, much to the dismay of Mutter; but then Opa convinced her that there were worse things a boy could be doing.

For the longest time they had tried to figure out why Hermann wasn't strong enough to hold himself up and walk on his own and Mutter had desperately gone from doctor to doctor seeking a cure, but given the state of medicine in 1930s Germany, they eventually came to grips with the fact that Hermann would have to use a wheelchair for whatever reason they didn't know. Religious Opa often wondered whether it was a punishment from God, and Mother was inclined to believe him. It wasn't until much later after the war, that Hermann would be diagnosed with muscular dystrophy. Hermann was categorized as a cripple and excused from the Hitler Jugend.

The boys' dad had died in a moped accident when Karl was only eight months old. It had been a gruesome accident: Mutter had arrived at the accident scene to witness her husband lying in the road with his severed leg lying tangential to his body in the middle of the street, blood everywhere. His moped had been hit by a speeding driver who cut a curve too short, instantly killing Karl Sr. and dragging his body for a while. After seeing the severed leg and her husband's body, Mutter refused to get near him and remained at a distance watching the spectacle of people trying to revive him. She just stood there helpless and distraught until his body was taken away. Eventually, Frau Mueller, a neighbor, walked Mutter home. Opa had to make the funeral arrangements. From then on, living with Opa was the only solution for the small family as they would have struggled on their own. Three years into the war, food was scares and the store shelves were mostly empty; hence three generations living together was very common.

Karl knew his dad from a few old black-and-white pictures, but mostly from the comforting stories Mutter would tell. His dad had been a hard worker and for his multitude of services was a well-liked man in the county. Karl secretly often yearned for him, especially before the war when he saw the neighborhood kids playing with their dads or even just watching his friends interact with their fathers: arms wrapped around or holding hands. But Karl learned early on to control his emotions and feelings; he knew telling Mutter about how much he missed having a father would make her upset. When all of his friends' dads were later recruited, it made him feel no longer as inadequate in comparison: he and his friends then together shared the common bond of being fatherless.

Opa ran his own carpentry business out of the house. Years ago, Karl's Uropa (great-grandfather) had turned the basement level of his modest brick-house into a carpentry shop or "*Schreinerei.*" It had a separate downstairs entrance and hanging still in front of it was the original sign used by the great-grandfather, distinguished by the old symbols of the carpentry guild: a carpenter's plane, a square and a compass.

The carpentry connected to a large back storage room and housed an assortment of wood and tools: one hand-drill, three axes, two saws, three chisels, two squares, one level, one wrench, a large dresser filled with all types of nails, screws, screwdrivers and hammers, and a variety of paint sitting beside it, along with any other wood supply one could think of.

His maternal uncle Joseph had helped out in the family's carpentry until October 1939, when Joseph was ordered to join the war. One rainy morning, a caravan of Wehrmacht trucks idled outside in the streets, standing ready for the new recruits. Along with neighbors, relatives and friends, Opa, Mutter, Karl, Hans and Hermann in his wheelchair, all stood outside in the drizzle, looking on helplessly as Uncle Joseph, along with others disappeared into the back of the trucks. Then together they waved their sad and destitute good-byes as the truck caravan disappeared into the horizon.

They hadn't heard from Uncle Joseph since that unforgettable autumn morning. Too many times to count, Mutter inquired about any type of news of her brother at the local *Gruppenhaus,* the makeshift city hall, to no avail. She was told over and over not to worry, that everything was all right, and that if anything were wrong, she would have heard. But everyone knew that something had to be wrong, not hearing from Uncle Joseph at all.

The flamboyant neighbor lady, Frau Mueller living diagonally across the street, received two letters from her husband, each one a year apart, providing her with renewed hope. He was fighting at the Russian front in Moscow, he said, and he hoped to be back soon. Hauptmann Mueller had been recruited the same day as Uncle Joseph and Mutter had asked Frau Mueller if her husband had mentioned anything in the letters about her brother, but while Hauptmann Mueller complained that he hadn't received any letters from his frau, even though she had sent at least 20 letters to him, there was no mention of Uncle Joseph. What had become of Uncle Joseph and all those letters Frau Mueller had sent? Why was her husband not receiving them? Frau Mueller inquired at the local city hall, but that day she was told "to consider herself lucky if they don't stop by with other news" which she considered so heartless that she vowed to never return there again. She continued to write the letters, but asked a friend of hers to drop them off at the city hall in hopes that one of the letters would make it to her dearly missed husband.

She then never heard from him again, and questions about Uncle Joseph's whereabouts were never answered. Yet, the Mueller and Elheusch families never gave up hope.

Karl, early on, had found his passion while tinkering with wood in Opa's carpentry. Whether building a dresser drawer, repairing the roof of a neighbor's house, or fixing a window frame, he could do it all.

Karl and Hans were filling in as the breadwinners for their father and uncle. Their circumstances forced them to mature early. Most stores couldn't keep daily staples in stock. Not only was the family relying on Hans herding the neighbors' cows but also sometimes they shared some of their modest potato harvest in exchange for the farmer's eggs, flour or other small items. They would borrow the farmer's plow horse each spring to dig the furrows on the small field they owned, located next to Opa's house, so the boys together with Mutter could plant the potatoes evenly spaced. Continuously they would water and weed the small field, watching the green sprouts grow with excitement and a few months later they would harvest their modest crop. It was a lot of bending, tiring but full-filling work, because they knew the bounty would feed them for a few months or they could use it for trade. The furniture they built or repaired, mostly for neighbors, additionally provided them with an income during these hard times, whether the payment came in the form of Marken or other supplies.

Under the direction of Opa and Mutter, Karl quickly became very proficient in wood-working, and while they eagerly did all of the necessary work, Karl took more of a liking to carpentry than Hans did to herding. Karl viewed the hard labor associated with chopping the trees, shaving the tree trunks and then cutting them to size as necessary up-front work to gather the needed material to build and create the furniture. For him, carpentry was nearly an art: he enjoyed the sawing, measuring, chiseling, and refinishing of the wood to create a final and unique product.

The carpentry of the Elheusch family was already well known in the area from decades of quality work, and now Karl was following into the footsteps of proud carpenters. Word of their fine craft continued to spread. Customers and even non-customers in their small village were aware of the unique furniture that Opa, Mutter, and then Karl were crafting.

Karl's dream was to earn the official title of carpenter someday, with a certificate to back it up, like Opa's or Dad's whose hung on the white carpentry walls. Opa at one point had thought to remove Karl Sr.'s certificate, but Mutter had insisted it remain. Karl would need to take additional carpentry classes and become an apprentice in the neighboring city's carpentry shop for a couple of years before getting this final "Schreiner Meister" ("master of carpentry") certificate, but while he had started on it, there were so many reasons he couldn't finish this apprenticeship: Opa needed his help in the shop, and mostly, the Hitler Jugend didn't allow for those plans. For now Opa's continued "on the job" training would have to do.

Karl dropped out of school in the beginning of 8th grade, deciding that helping out in Opa's carpentry was much more important than listening to the propaganda he was being taught in school or at the Hitler Jugend meetings. "Propaganda" was Mutter's most used word those days; she insisted the Nazis were spreading falsities to the naïve masses.

Mutter was adamantly opposed to everything that had to do with Hitler and the war. She knew from listening to the forbidden channels on her radio that the Allies were closing in and that too many lives were being lost daily. She was against Hitler from the time she first heard anything about him. She never bought into the Nazi ideology and the nationalistic belief it was spreading. She despised the censorship the Nazis imposed on her, like telling her which books she could read, or what could be written in the newspaper. She was a practicing Catholic, but only in the secrecy of her own home.

She remained resentful of the regime and missed the days when she could listen to anything on the radio without censorship. Not that there were many Volkssender channels to choose from then, but there were no restrictions and no threats if one listened to any desired channel or read anything that was available. Propaganda minister Joseph Goebbels would refer to the foreign media as "Luegenpresse" ("Lying Press"). According to the propaganda, everyone but the Nazis was lying.

Opa was also a very staunch Catholic, though church masses no longer took place. All the Catholic priests had vanished or stopped practicing. Opa was getting more and more withdrawn, mostly just working in his small carpentry, with the boys being the only highlights in his days.

Mutter and Opa were appalled at how the Jews were being treated and everything they heard about them being singled out and blamed for felt wrong, and it was absolutely not right to treat another religion that way. There was one Jewish family – the Morgenthau family – residing in their village that owned a small jewelry shop. One day a sign was put in front of their store that read, *"Deutsche wehrt euch, kauft nicht von Juden."* (Germans defend yourselves, don't buy from Jews). Then, the store was shuttered, with a huge Star of David painted on it, along with a "Closed" sign.

Mutter said that it all reminded her too much about all the stories Opa had told her about World War I, another futile war started by ill-advised German leadership. In 1914 the German army had invaded neutral Belgium and northern France and executed thousands of Belgian and French civilians. Opa, who had lost an eye in battle during World War I, repeatedly told tales about the senselessness and cruelties of that war, and the needless human sacrifices that came with it. He was against this second war and convinced his daughter and grandsons that it was just another worthless fight, started by this lunatic Hitler.

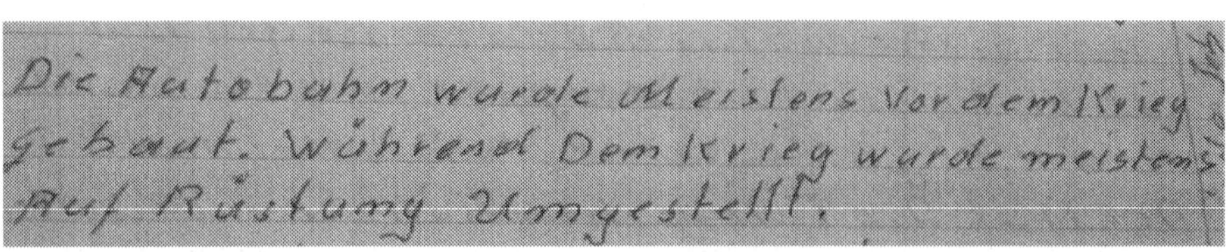
Die Autobahn wurde Meistens Vor dem Krieg
gebaut. Während Dem Krieg wurde meistens
Auf Rüstung Umgestellt.

Example of Karl's writing[iv]

They knew that the main reason much of the German population was initially smitten by Hitler was that his propaganda fed into the dissatisfaction of the largely unemployed population. Over and over, Hitler blamed the Jews for the strong sanctions following World War I, and the subsequent decline of the German economy. Hitler ordered the autobahn construction before the war, which then employed many. Because he improved German lives, many considered him a hero, but he never missed the chance to blame the Jews for Germany's demise since WWI. "*Hitler knew what to do about the unemployment and fixed it, we can trust him, hence he must also be right about the Jewish problem,*" was the basic logic. But eventually, mostly all civilian factories were turned into defense mills and war fighter construction machines, and it was too late for the German population to affect change.

At the dinner table one night Mutter was especially outraged. "These poor kids! It's just horrible!" Distraught she went on to tell her sons what she had heard on the radio, the Volkssender.

"Last week, three college students at Munich University tried to resist the Hitler regime."

She now whispered, afraid to be heard through the brick walls of their house. "They passed around leaflets at their university to open people's eyes about Hitler. They were a brother and sister team, Geschwister Scholl was their name, along with their friend. Apparently a janitor saw them dropping the leaflets and without hesitation snitched them out. The young students were swiftly prosecuted, and within a day executed. Their punishment is to serve as an example of what will happen to anyone who stands against the regime."

She sighed. "Those students were right to protest and hand out those leaflets!"

"But look at their punishment!" Opa said, somberly. "It doesn't pay to be a hero!"

"Right! Your life is not worth it!" agreed Mutter.

At the time, Mutter continued to come up with many excuses for her sons so they could avoid attending the required Hitler Jugend meetings. It was more important that Karl focused on improving his carpentry skills; and Hans' extra income was needed to sustain the family.

One night shortly after the Munich incident, there was a loud knock at the front door. Startled, everyone looked toward the door at the end of the foyer. Who could be here this late? Without waiting for an answer, tall Albert Wuest, a neighborhood boy, forced the door open and stormed in.

"*Guten Abend!* (Good evening!)" Albert, with his greasy brown hair sleeked to the side and pimples all over his face, strutted forward into the kitchen. Wearing his freshly creased Hitler Youth uniform and high, shiny, black boots, he moved around as if it were his own home. He had been to their house many times and felt very comfortable here.

"I was sent here because Hans and Karl missed yet another meeting. As you all well know, all boys and girls have to attend all required meetings. It is the law; it went into effect March 1939!" Dramatically he pointed his finger in the air to emphasize his point. "But not only is it now required by law, there are many reasons and benefits why your sons can't miss any more meetings, Frau Elheusch," Albert demanded from Mutter in his crackly, adolescent voice, staring directly at her. His father had become a member of the Sturmstaffel (SS), and Albert was a stout follower of the Hitler Jugend, rising quickly to a leadership rank. His strong belief in the Nazi ideology was clear.

Karl studied Albert's face as he continued his rant. Two years older, Albert had been one of Karl's playmates just a few years back. Hans and Albert had been in the same grade. Together with other neighborhood kids, like Michael Morgenthau, they used to play soccer in their back yard with Hermann as the goalie. That was something Hermann could do – he could sit in the grass and let his body fall side to side, guarding the narrow make-shift goal, the imaginary posts marked by chunks of wood. Despite his handicap, Hermann had always been part of the group: Karl, Hans, Albert, Michael and Martin. They raced each other in the neighborhood streets, and Hermann would be the one giving the signal "Auf den Platz, fertig, los" ("ready, set, go") and refereeing if the race was ever close. They ran through the wheat fields with Hermann looking out for any grownups. Their races dismayed the farmers, who often complained to the parents to keep their kids out of the fields, because trampled wheat plants would be impossible to harvest. The boys also often explored the nearby creek and woods just down the hills from their houses.

One day they were hiking along the creek at the bottom of the hill, stopping to poke at the tadpoles with twigs, when Albert grabbed a frog, pulled out a pocket knife and cut off the frog's legs. "Yum! Frog legs!" Albert had exclaimed, laughing, proudly holding up the cut up frog by one leg and stuffing the cut up raw frog leg into his mouth.

"Ewwww - That is just cruel, Albert," Karl had tried to intervene and stop Albert from cutting up the next frog. The two boys wrestled, with Karl trying to take Albert's pocket knife. In the shuffle, Albert cut Karl's thigh and then escaped Karl's grip and laughed the most *schadenfrohes* (gloating) laugh. "What are you going to do? You can't stop me," he teased Karl, holding up the knife as he ran off to look for more frogs.

Blood was seeping through Karl's khaki pant leg from the cut. He tried to cover up the wound with his hand to stop the bleeding. Dejectedly, Karl turned to Michael, nodding toward the hill. "Let's go back; let's not be associated with him." Red cheeked and upset, Michael and Karl headed home to Mutter. Karl downplayed the wound as a result of accidentally cutting himself. Mutter was suspicious, but she was focused on taking Karl to the doctor, where he got stiches to close the deep gash. The doctor said that if the wound had been just a few millimeters farther right, it could have hit the femoral artery, and been life threatening.

Karl had avoided Albert since that incident.

Here two years later, in his overly starched brown Hitler Jugend (youth) uniform shirt and black pants, with the black swastika stitched on a white and red patch wrapped around his left arm, Albert was pacing back and forth in their kitchen, causing the old wooden kitchen floors in Opa's house to creak with every one of his strides, as if the wooden planks were complaining about his presence. Albert went on with his demands: "They cannot miss another meeting!" This was nothing new, it was the same message Karl heard on Mutter's radio, when she listened to the Nazi news: all youth needed to attend the Hitler Jugend. Mutter had talked about all the brainwashed people in the past, and "Albert is definitely brainwashed," Karl was convinced.

Mutter knew that she would be held responsible for her sons' Hitler Jugend attendance. Missing the meetings was a criminal offense, punishable by a fine of 150 marks or imprisonment. Karl and his brother had enjoyed being members of the Catholic Youth Club, and resented the fact that after joining the Hitler Jugend they were ordered to denounce the Catholic Youth membership. They no longer were allowed to take part in any religious activities, or else face serious punishment.

"As you know the Hitler Jugend law came into effect on 25. March 1939, and it includes the Jugenddienstpflicht (youth-service duty) requirement. In the Hitler Jugend, we will make sure the youths know the purpose of the Third Reich. All younger members are mentored and trained by smart, young adults who will help implement the goals of our Fuehrer…they will help build the "1000-year Reich." Albert rattled on.

Karl watched Albert's every move, listening to him carefully and reading every cue. "*He is wasting his time here*," Karl remained convinced that Mutter would come up with the right explanations as to why they couldn't attend all the meetings: The carpentry and the cows need tending to.

After a while longer of attentively listening to Albert's rambling, Karl was getting impatient and couldn't wait for him to leave. Mutter had made carrot soup with a few potatoes added to it; the pot of soup was sitting on the dining room table and the steam that had been rising from it had now stopped. And after dinner, Karl still needed to help Hans clean out the carpentry as they had promised Opa.

"Sorry, I need to go. I have to clean the carpentry." Karl couldn't take it any longer, got up, and tried to excuse himself.

"No, you need to hear this!" Albert barked back so intensely he stopped Karl mid-movement. Annoyed, Karl slowly sat back down, staring back at Albert. "*Who does this guy think he is, just because he is in this uniform?*" Karl was now very agitated, but bit his tongue and remained quiet.

"I need to know that you will attend all the meetings. Nothing is more important than supporting the goal of our Fuehrer. We need everyone's help, whether 12 years or 60 years. Promise me that you won't miss another meeting. Promise!" and then Albert lowered his voice, and leaning in closely to be on eye level with Mutter, he paused for a split second and then whispered emphatically: """....because I don't want to have to turn you all in!"

Karl looked at Mutter, who seemed to have turned a bit paler with now a very weary look on her face. He stepped forward reflexively, trying to defend Mutter, aghast that Albert had just threatened her like that. She in turn quickly motioned Karl to stay back. Then slowly, she got up and held Albert's gaze, then annunciating every word she directed at him: "I've known you since the day you were born. I babysat you and even changed your diapers, and your mom, in turn, has watched Hans, Karl and Hermann. You have played together and you have eaten many meals here. And today you are here to threaten me?" Her voice ended in a higher pitch.

Albert looked away for a moment as if to digest what he just heard, but then he turned and stared back directly at Mutter holding her gaze, resolved and sterner than before he responded: "Frau Elheusch, the past is completely irrelevant. It doesn't matter what happened then. While I appreciate what you did for me and my family, it is the past. We now have to look to the future of this country. We have our calling. We need to implement the orders the Fuehrer gives us. If you don't want to follow those orders, I have to report you! It is the law, and I am here to make sure the law is being followed!"

With that, the room fell silent. Maria, stunned, sat back down in her chair. Her mouth was slightly open. All her resistance seemed to have crumbled at this point. She looked defeated. "Alright, I'll make sure they will be at all the meetings!" Now tired, she kept her gaze down, as if she didn't want to face Albert any longer. Albert had won. Karl could barely hide his surprise.

"But Mutter, what about all the work around here?" Hans tried to protest.

She hissed at him "You heard Albert. He is right; we need to support the Fuehrer. Now you both promise Albert you will go to all the meetings!"

Karl and Hans looked at Mutter dumbfounded. Never in the past had she asked them to support the Fuehrer. Karl was suspicious, but her stern stare piercing at them quickly made them realize that they had better agree.

"We promise," they both obliged nearly in unison.

A satisfied grin covered Albert's face. He got what he wanted. "Good, I needed to hear that. You will not regret it. There is so much you will learn about our wonderful Fuehrer and his plans. You will be so impressed."

Then he scanned the room, slowly, as if he suddenly remembered to look for something: "And where is his book?"

Immediately they knew he was talking about "Mein Kampf," Hitler's manifesto.

"I have it, I can get it," Mutter responded, even more annoyed at the personal questions.

"Mein Kampf" of course needs to be out in the open. You should have it sitting out here in the open so any of your visitors can see it, and of course your boys can read it anytime they feel like reading Hitler's great work."

"Go get it!"

Mutter's cheeks now appeared even more caved in, her narrow set green eyes squinted, it was clear she was very frustrated at this point, though she reluctantly got up after taking in Albert's determined, matter-of-fact expression once more. Everyone in the kitchen stayed quiet, while she slowly climbed up the squeaky wooden stairs to her bedroom. Once there she pulled open the drawer of her pressed wood old night desk: in it were a few of the books that the Nazis had handed to the kids in school or had dropped off here at their house. On the top was a children's book called "*Trau keinem Fuchs auf grüner Heid und keinem Jud bei seinem Eid!"* (Translation: "Trust No Fox on his Green Heath And No Jew on his Oath"). She had kept all these types of books in her night desks: when they were little she purposely had avoided reading any of them to her boys, and now that they were older, they had no interest in reading this "garbage," as they all referred to it. Hidden under the children books she found the red covered "Mein Kampf," by Adolf Hitler. Quickly she grabbed it and rushed back down the steps.

"I'll keep it here!" she placed the book in the middle of the kitchen table in an attempt to appease Albert.

"It looks brand-new!" he picked it up and flipped through it, his black eyebrows rolled up in surprise.

"I am taking good care of it!" Mutter defended the lack of use of that book, which had become the "bible" of the National Socialist German Workers' Party (NAZIs).

"Alright, well then, make sure your boys read it, they will be quizzed about it at the Hitler Jugend!" Albert ordered again. Mutter just nodded at this point.

"Come on now! Let's do the Hitler salute" Albert seemed content, he angled his arm at 45 degrees, bellowed "Heil Hitler!" and encouraged the boys to copy him. They, in turn, reluctantly and almost embarrassed, followed suit. Clicking his heels, right hand extended, Albert left them with a second loud "Heil Hitler!" He marched out the door stepping high and full of pride.

As soon as Albert slammed the door behind him, Karl ran up to it, turned the heavy iron key, and locked it.

"We need to remember to keep this door locked!" he exhaled, then turned around and questioned: "Mutter?" He studied her face.

"Sssshhhhhh," she put her fingers on her lips and lowered her voice. "Remember the Morgenthaus? We didn't know what happened to them? They had been hiding out at Mr. Morgenthau's in-laws house ever since their jewelry store was closed where they used to live upstairs. Well, Frau Mueller told me that the SS has arrested the entire family there and took them away Sunday evening. Albert's father was leading the SS pack in the arrest. Frau Mueller hears the reason they gave is because they are Jewish. That was their only reason! That's all they needed for an arrest!"

Karl was now worried for his friend Michael: "What will happen to him, his parents and Anna, Michael's sister?"

"I am not sure. Frau Morgenthau is a former Sommer, she is not Jewish, she just married a Jewish guy, so they might just let her and her kids go. Of course they should let him go too, but she has a better chance!"

Karl kept prying "Is there anything we can do for them?"

"No, Frau Mueller doesn't know where they took them. There are rumors about labor camps, but nobody seems to know more details or if they do, nobody wants to talk about it."

Mutter then deflected Karl's concern for Michael by going back to the topic at hand: "Albert is not to be trusted; his entire family is not to be trusted, they are one of the many enforcing these laws. It is a bad sign that he was here. We need to just do exactly what he says. I don't want any of us to be arrested and end up in a camp; we need to stick together, go along with it for now." And then she whispered even lower. "We don't have to do it for much longer. The Allied soldiers are coming, I heard it on the radio. Hitler doesn't have much time left."

Hans scolded: "Mutter, you know you are not allowed to listen to those radio stations. What if we get caught? We all get arrested!"

Karl also worried, chimed in in support. "Mutter, yes, please stop listening to those stations!"

"It doesn't matter. I am careful about the stations, you know I only play them at the lowest volume. Lately I have been putting a sheet over my head when I listen." She chuckles at herself for a split second, but then quickly became serious again. "You have to be more careful about yourselves! Go to those meetings, agree to what they say. Just pretend you agree; it's not for much longer."

The boys wanted to explain to her that her radio signals could be traced, but the conversation was over.

Chapter 4:

The Furniture Order

Using the old broom, Karl feverishly swept wood chips and saw dust off the worn carpentry floor. The broom's bristles were so sparse it took Karl repeated strokes to get the chips into a pile.

It was nearing the end of another long work day, and Opa was sitting down at the other end of the room sanding an unfinished chair, which he was restoring for one of the neighbors. Now in his 70s, Opa's legs were too weak to allow him to stand for too long, and it was too difficult for him to bend down, so having the chair in his lap seemed to be the most practical way of getting the sanding done.

Suddenly, and without a knock, the downstairs store door ripped open and the rusty bell hanging off it on a worn-out string rattled louder than usual against the wooden frame, as if to complain about the unexpected interruption. The SS soldier appearing in the door frame was in his late 30s, with sculpted features, high cheek bones, and black hair, cut short. He was approximately the same height as Karl, who now at 16 was 5-foot-8. The soldier's dark piercing eyes glared at them.

Stopping mid-work, Opa and Karl both startled, stared back at the unexpected intruder this late in the afternoon.

Recognizing the officer as one of the SS's, Opa gasped nervously, noticeable only to Karl, and leaned back into the shadow of the room where the window's late afternoon sunlight didn't reach, while Karl dropped his broom and immediately jumped to attention and saluted.

"Heil Hitler," was the mutual salute, Karl's and the soldier's heels clicking. The Hitler Jugend training, which he and Hans had been attending diligently since Albert threatened them in their kitchen over a year ago, had taught him this required response: the right arm had to be slanted and stretched out at eye level, with the hand flat and facing down. Not using the extended arm signal, along with the greeting would have been considered a grave disrespect, chargeable with immediate arrest. Karl had long learned to read the ranks by the uniform insignia.

"May I help you, Herr Major?" asked Karl, only lowering his right arm from the salute after the officer did so.

"Major Hildenberg!" He announced his name in a deep, raspy voice: "I need an oak desk!" he demanded, without any further introduction. At the same time, the Major took off his black leather gloves and tapped his right hand's fingertips with them as he spoke. His appearance, with his shiny boots and pressed uniform, was impeccable. Karl and Opa stared at him in anticipation as the Major continued. "I need you to build me an oak desk and a matching oak chair. It needs to meet specific requirements. It is for a special visitor to the town. He is expected here Friday, in one week! We need a day to transport it and set it up in our office, so…," he hesitated to allow himself time to add the days. "Can you have it all done by next Wednesday?"

"*One week isn't nearly enough time for building an oak desk,*" Karl reacted to himself in panic, but glancing at his Opa and seeing him nod energetically, Karl answered quickly: "Yes, Sir. Of course, Herr Major! Can we hear the specs? What design do you have in mind?"

"Sketch it as I describe it! I want to make sure we have a mutual agreement. There is no room for misunderstanding," the Major ordered.

Opa shuffled as fast as he could toward the desk near the wall and frantically opened the old wooden drawers, not daring to turn his back to the SS officer as he pulled out a "Faber" pencil. The Major sensed Opa's uneasiness and kept his dark brown, mistrusting eyes focused on Opa's every move. With his arthritis-stricken and bent hands, Opa handed the pencil and paper to Karl, who then cautiously motioned to the Major to have a seat at the wooden table that was planted in the middle of the small carpentry. Karl also rushed over to it, and with his sleeves, quickly wiped off a few specks of sawdust. "Opa, I will need a ruler," Karl nodded at the old wooden ruler visible in the drawer. Opa quickly obliged and handed it to Karl.

Major Hildenberg took off his light-grey military cap and placed it at the end of the table and then dragged the old chair up to it. He sat down with one of his legs extended to the side, appearing to be ready to jump up at a moment's notice.

Karl sat down on the opposite side of the Major, glancing down at the piece of paper, gesturing with the pencil to show his eagerness to start drawing. "I am ready, Herr Major," Karl said.

"The oak desk's front edge should be the shape of a wave," the Major's large tan hand made a long horizontal up and down wave motion: "The front of the desk needs to be 2 meters wide and the sides 1 meter deep." Karl's eyes widened ever so slightly as he tried to imagine the unusually shaped desk, but he remained quiet and tried hard to keep his facial expressions neutral. He fiercely worked to recreate the Major's thoughts on paper, sketching it as best as he could, while the Major demanded he measure and draw the desk to size.

"Draw it to a 10 cm : 1 m ratio," he demanded.

"Also, I want the oak desk in black. Black lacquer. It needs to be nice and shiny!"

Karl continued to wonder *"Black? Why would anyone paint an oak desk black? Why not leave the natural color of the oak and at most seal it? It will look like a piano,"* though Karl wouldn't dare to question the Major and continued to draw the desk model to meet the design, as the Major watched Karl's every mark, requiring him to modify the shapes here and there. Karl used the old wooden ruler to draw the unusual shaped desk to size.

The soldier continued to describe his demands: The legs should have the same shape as the front of the desk – the shape of a wave." *"That surely will make things difficult!"* Karl thought but remained calm.

"The legs shall give enough room so anyone a bit heavier can comfortably push the chair under the desk and sit in it. Of course the chair color is to match the desk, so paint it black, also," the Major continued. "The back of the chairs also needs to be wave-shaped to match the desk's design."

"Of course," answered Karl, his disagreement starting to show ever so slightly.

The Major's eyes squinted at Karl. "Of course, what?" the Major immediately caught on.

“Of course, Herr Major. I am in agreement with you, and of course the table will be the same color as the desk,” Karl responded, softly appeasing the Major while staying head down.

After much erasing, clarifying and modifying, Karl finally came up with a draft of the unusual custom desk and chair design with which the Major finally seemed satisfied.

Then the Major’s eyebrows rose. “When are you starting on this? I want to see progress as it’s being built. I need to make sure it is exactly as we want it,” and with his black gloves, the Major pointed and tapped to the rough sketch of the furniture outline on the piece of paper, with Karl still feverishly adding finishing touches, smoothing out edges, blowing away the eraser slivers and adding final lines.

Before Karl could look up to answer, the Major repeated his demand agitated: “This date cannot be missed!”

Karl jumped up saluting: “If you permit me, Herr Major, I am very sure we have the wood, but let me check the back storage area to be one-hundred percent sure we have the specific size oak wood needed for this order.” Without waiting for approval Karl grabbed the drawing and headed for the shed.

“Well, you’d better, or...” before the Major could finish, Karl had already opened the door to the adjacent wood storage.

The Major mumbled to himself, but Opa couldn’t make out what he said and instead chose to put the chair back on his lap and continued sanding it.

Karl had one large piece of oak in mind, but before fully committing to that important deadline, he needed to measure the size of it to make sure they could accommodate the unusual order.

The heavy door to the dimly lit storage room was squeaking eerily as Karl opened it and penetrating smell of wood immediately surrounded him. "*I need some drops to oil this door*," Karl thought, as he had so many times before. It was all so much easier when Uncle Joseph was still with them. Because Karl had lost his father so early, his uncle had been a father figure to him, and at times like these he missed him more than ever.

Karl looked through the stacks of oak. The wood was neatly lined up, stacked by size and organized by type and the familiar smell of wood resin was hovering in the air. He liked the smell. It was something he grew up with. Using Opa's old tractor, they had pulled the trunks from the forest on the 10 acres of land owned by Opa. In Opa's backyard, using their saw, together with his brother Hans, Karl had cut the huge tree trunks into nice-sized sheets before moving them in here. This was hard labor and a lot of work, but Karl didn't mind it. Sometimes Michael would help out, making the chores more bearable and fun, especially because Michael was not only a hard worker but also had a great sense of humor lightening the mood with his jokes and shenanigans.

The wood, however, was now starting to run low. There was not much stored wood left until summer and when Karl finally found the perfect oak pieces in front of him, he was relieved. They were from the one oak tree that took Hans, Michael and Opa, and even Mutter, days to chop up and store away. It was an old oak tree saved for a special occasion. Karl had dreamed of showing off his carpentry skills to the world using these huge chunks of oak someday. "Now," he sighed, "it will be used for this Major's furniture order." Taking out his meter stick, he measured the beautiful oak's length and width. He touched it to feel and verify its quality, and roughly measured it to verify it again, even though it was separate from the pre-measured piles of wood and even though experience and his keen eye knew the size would be adequate for the Major's order. Karl held up the drawing to study it again and to imagine how he would shape the wood chunks into the requested design. It would take thick boards to make the table top. He recognized this was an incredibly important order: important to Opa, his family, to their livelihood. The Munich events and the Morgenthau's disappearance were just two of the many examples that had everyone scared to death.

He closed the wooden door to the shed and returned to the front room, where Opa and the Major were both pretending the other was not present. They had not spoken a word.

With relief apparent on his face, Karl assured: "Jawohl, Herr Major. We can have the order ready in time." Karl beamed and quickly glanced confidently over at Opa, who was still sanding but watching it all unfold from the back of the room, determined to stay uninvolved, though Karl noticed a slight exhale coming from Opa as he leaned forward.

The Major's lips formed a quick smile, so fleeting, that Karl later doubted it had ever been there.

Major Hildenberg officially signed the sketch, scribbled the due date and made Karl sign it: This paper was to be considered a contract, and the Major repeated that he would be back in the next couple days to witness progress. He added, in a low but undoubtedly threatening tone, leaning in toward Karl, as if Opa was not supposed to hear the intimation, looking eye to eye: "I expect quality furniture. If you deliver in time, and to my satisfaction, I will award you. If the order is not ready in time, there will be consequences!"

Quickly saluting, the Major then turned 180-degrees and strutted out. Karl made an attempt to return the salute, but the Major had turned around so quickly that Karl dropped his hand mid-salute – it was unimportant once the Major had left.

With the threatening words still hanging in the air, Karl stood there almost paralyzed, staring at the door, the bell still vibrating. They were both imagining the types of consequences the Major was referring to. Opa frantically broke the silence: "Karl, let's get started on this now! I know it's late, but can you get Hans, so you two can drag the oak in here, and we can get started?" Karl could feel Opa's anxiety.

"Ja!" Karl quickly ran upstairs past Mutter, who in her grey apron, was in the kitchen cutting potatoes and preparing soup with the few ingredients she could find. "Where is Hans, Mutter?" he asked hastily, scanning the kitchen for his brother. "He's in his room," she responded, looking up from cutting because she could sense the worry in Karl's voice. "What's wrong?"

Without an answer, Karl darted upstairs to find Hans lying in bed reading the Bible, underlying noteworthy verses as he did so often, completely oblivious to his surroundings.

"Hans, put that away! You need to hide it!! An SS Major was just here and ordered an oak desk."

Hans quickly covered the Bible under his blanket.

"He left. He wants a desk that's wave shaped, 4 m x 2.5 m, black lacquered with a matching chair. And it all has to be ready to be delivered by next week Wednesday!"

Hans' eyes widened. "Wait. Slow down. That's impossible!"

"Opa and I both will have to work around the clock (um die Uhr). We'll just need to get it done. You need to help, too. We want to get started right away."

Grasping the urgency, Hans immediately jumped out of bed, slid into his slippers, and followed Karl downstairs. They heard Mutter calling, "Soup's ready in a minute!" as they passed by the kitchen.

Hans quickly responded with, "Mutter, bitte bring it downstairs, we don't have time to sit down and eat."

Karl was determined to deliver that furniture order in time. He snatched the sketch off the table where he had left it, and with it they marched into the back room.

"You grab this end and I this!" he ordered Hans, pointing at the oak and handed the sketch to Opa, who had followed to oversee it all, to hold on to it.

Meticulously measuring and sawing the pieces, sweat dripping into their eyes, holding the pieces and sizing them up against each other, Karl and Opa began to build the unusual shaped oak desk. Karl didn't hammer, but instead carefully chiseled the nails into the wood. He wanted the desk and chair to be of especially high quality. Their lives depended on it. They worked until the early morning hours when finally, completely exhausted, they went to sleep.

****

Karl dreaded and despised each Hitler Jugend meeting. Especially that week, he much preferred to be building any piece of furniture in Opa's little carpentry. And now he had a desk to complete. But he had no choice but to attend one of the many required Hitler Jugend gatherings.

Sitting in half circles in their meeting hall, they heard that day from Albert, who was leading Karl's group, about the *Spitzel* (spies) who turned in anyone who said just the slightest negative word about Hitler. Albert was recruiting Spitzels (spies) today, but Karl didn't want to be part of it. Albert then told the story of two students who had written up their teacher preaching against the regime. He now needed one of the Hitler Jugend boys to sit in one of this teacher's classes to catch him fresh-handed.

"Karl, you haven't been to school in a while. He wouldn't suspect you!" Albert taunted him to sign up for the spy work.

"No, I have a furniture order from a Major that I need to work on. We have a tight deadline for it, next Wednesday," was Karl's excuse, which to Karl's relief Albert quickly accepted. Everyone knew a Major's order was to be taken very seriously.

That moment, Karl was actually thankful to the Major for placing this order, because it gave him that acceptable excuse. Karl would do anything to avoid becoming like the janitor who ratted out the Scholz brother and sister for dropping leaflets, and who was ultimately responsible for their execution. "*How could this janitor live with himself? Those young students with a bright future beheaded only because they stood up for their beliefs!*" The tragic story of the Scholz brother and sister was one of many that continued to haunt Karl.

Who would the poor boy be; selected to spy on this teacher to turn him in? Karl wished he could warn that teacher, but there were so many spies everywhere, and even getting near him at that point would be too risky.

Then came the outdoor portion of the Hitler Jugend meeting and it was time for marching practice. They were ordered to march to the nearest forest, they lined up and were lead along. The muffled sounds of marching steps and chanting became increasingly louder, then droning, disrupting the calm of this beautiful fall display in the countryside of Southern Germany. A group of *Rotkehlchen* (robins) who hadn't started their migration yet, was sipping the water in the small creek that had formed from an earlier rain shower. As the troops got closer the birds scurried.

It was October of 1944, five years into World War II. Now even taller and more muscular, Karl marched as part of his Troop B, stepping the goose-step, along with his teenage friends: kicking their stiff legs high in unison and down swiftly like synchronized robots. They marched with their right arms extended stiff to form the "Heil, Hitler" salute, guns holstered over their left shoulders, heads turned. Karl, with his red curls and hazel eyes, wore chiseled facial expressions that were cold and distant for a young man. His movements were mechanical and his mind was not present, though he became skilled in marching along, involuntarily, without any inner conviction, and joining in their chants:

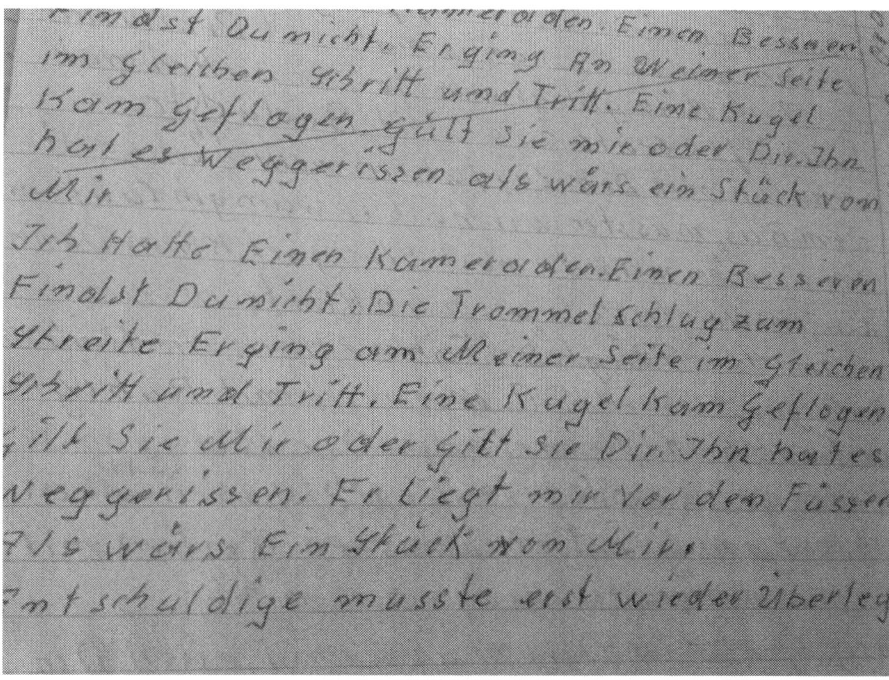

...[Kamer]aden. Einen Bessern
Findst Du nicht. Er ging An Meiner Seite
im Gleichen Schritt und Tritt. Eine Kugel
Kam Geflogen gilt Sie mir oder Dir. Ihn
hat es Weggerissen als wärs ein Stück von
Mir

Ich Hatte Einen Kameraden. Einen Besseren
Findst Du nicht. Die Trommel schlug zum
Streite Er ging an Meiner Seite im Gleichen
Schritt und Tritt. Eine Kugel kam Geflogen
Gilt Sie Mir oder gilt sie Dir. Ihn hat es
Weggerissen. Er liegt mir Vor den Füssen
Als wärs Ein Stück von Mir.

Entschuldige musste erst wieder überleg

Ich hatte einen Kameraden

Einen besseren findest du nicht
Die Trommel schlug zum Streite
Er ging an meiner Seite
im gleichen Schritt und Tritt
Eine Kugel kam geflogen
Gilt sie mir oder gilt sie dir
Ihn hat es weggerissen
Er liegt vor meinen Fuessen
als waer's ein Stueck von mir

Translation:
I once had a comrade
You will not find a better one
The drum called to battle
He walked at my side
In the same pace and step
A bullet came flying
Is it my turn or yours
He was ripped away
He lies at my feet
As if it was a part of me

As Karl's lips moved to the rhetoric of the chants his thoughts were with his frail Opa, Mutter and their carpentry. More than ever that day, Karl resented the drill, regimentation, political indoctrination, enforced uniformity, and lack of freedom and suppression of individual expression that the Hitler Youth membership imposed on him. Just when most kids wanted to experiment and wanted to become their own persons, the Hitler Youth demanded conformity to traditional values, thereby limiting any growth. Smoking, drinking, partying and sex were criminalized eventually, and the Nazis depended on Hitler Youth patrols to enforce the strict restrictions it placed on youthful behavior.

According to the Law for the Protection of Youth of March 9, 1940, young people under 18 were banned from the streets after dark and could not frequent bars, restaurants, cinemas, or other places of entertainment after nine o'clock in the evening if unaccompanied by an adult. In addition, it was made illegal for youths under 16 to smoke in public or to be served with spirits.[v]

Karl was not interested in getting drunk or smoking, but he just didn't like the numerous restrictions.

It was clear to him, that the Nazis didn't have any good intentions for Germany, and what really baffled Karl was that Hitler wasn't even German-born, but was born in Austria.

Marching and chanting along the German countryside, all Karl could imagine was the half-finished oak desk and chair, just as he had sketched it, and all the work that still had to get done.

".....a bullet came flying" they repeated the chants as they continued to goose-step.

"Who might that important visitor be the Major had referred to? Could it be that he was referring to the Fuehrer himself? The Fuehrer's headquarters were only 24 kilometers down the road from

their house, but he had heard that Hitler was hiding out in the Eagles Nest in Garmisch Partenkirchen. It could be easily possible that Hitler was coming. It seemed that it had to be a very important visitor for the Major to feel this strong about this exact date. But then again, he mentioned a heavy-set person. Who could it be?"

This furniture order would mean additional food on the table for Karl's family. The officer promised that Karl would be well compensated, if delivered in time. They had no other option, but to deliver.

Karl didn't believe in any of the words his lips were forming during the chants: *"Mein Vaterland, ueber alles..."* He heard himself say. "My Fatherland, above all of them...." Above all of the countries...? Why were they trying to instill the idea to them that Germany was superior to the rest of the world? What had happened to the country he grew up in, the country he knew? So much had changed since the war began five years earlier on September 3, 1939.

When they finally arrived at the forest, they were divided into two teams: one that would have to hide in the nearby woods and another that was tasked with searching for them. Karl despised these games, though he knew they were to gain important skills for defending themselves in a war, survivals skills necessary at this point of the war when Germany was retreating at all fronts and with many of the enemy soldiers already fighting in the forests. Karl that day purposely hid himself in the deep forest to just relax, trying to enjoy the calm of the nature as he sat behind a tree on the soft moss and would not return until he was sure it soon would be time for the entire group to march back. When he finally stepped out of the forest and re-joined his group, Albert gave him an all-knowing look, but for some reason decided not to belabor him. Karl looked away. Maybe Albert gave Karl a break because he must have known the pressure Karl was under to get this furniture order completed in time. The group marched back, and finally they were dismissed from the mandatory Saturday Hitler Jugend drills. Karl raced home in his heavy, black Hitler Jugend boots and once inside without a greeting he hollered "Mutter, can you bring the soup downstairs again, I have to continue working on the 'Major desk,' " as it came to be called, and quickly he disappeared into the carpentry shop.

Chapter 5

SS

After having feverishly worked on the "Major desk" for a few days, Karl started to feel confident that the order would be ready by the Wednesday deadline. The Major was scheduled to personally check again on progress the next day, and Karl expected that he would be happy with the progress so far. The piece of oak already had the beautiful majestic wave shape, exactly the dimensions the Major had asked for, and it was turning out to look more exquisite than Karl could have imagined.

It was close to midnight, and although exhausted, Karl was lying in bed wide awake. He should have been asleep, between the Hitler Jugend gatherings and the marching outside all day, then the continued sanding, hammering and chiseling of the desk; but all the stories floating in his mind were keeping him awake. His worried thoughts again were with the Scholl siblings, the young students who spoke up against Hitler and were executed over a year ago now. They were only kids, only a year or two older than his oldest brother, Hermann. Karl also worried about the teacher whom some of his comrades in the Hitler Jugend had turned in. What will happen to him?

He thought of the others who tried to speak up or had gone as far as try to assassinate Hitler, such as Claus Schenk Graf von Stauffenberg. Claus, together with others, had attempted to kill Hitler this past July 1944. With Hitler dead, Graf had hoped they could remove the Nazi Party from power. How did the attempt fail? Karl laid there imagining how it all went wrong. He had heard bits and pieces from others in the Hitler Jugend; unfortunately, Hitler was only barely injured in this assassination attempt. How did Hitler continue to escape these attacks? Expeditiously, Stauffenberg was executed by firing squad. Karl didn't know how they had traced the attack back to Stauffenberg, but it was clear there were enough Spitzels everywhere and nobody could be trusted. Karl wished he were older so he could help more, he was just 16 years old then, without any power. If he was older, he would support any freedom fighters. He imagined how he would succeed helping with the assassination. Somebody needed to finally stop Hitler.

Karl laid there tossing and turning, wondering what it would mean for Germany and to his family, if this war were finally over, or if the assassination attempts would have been successful. Or better yet, what if Hitler had been accepted by that art school he applied to a few times? Or if Hitler had been killed during his service in World War I? So many ifs, Karl could only dream of. Karl despised Hitler for so many reasons; also if it weren't for Hitler and his regime, Karl would now be finishing his carpentry apprenticeship at the renowned Nuernberg Schreinerei (carpentry). Although Opa was very skilled in teaching him the basics, Karl wanted to gain the newest woodcarving skills that Opa could not teach him. Karl sighed at the lost opportunity, and his thoughts now moved to his Jewish friend, Michael Morgenthau. He had lost all contact with him. Still nobody knew where the family had been taken. Hopefully, he would hear from him someday soon. He then thought about his uncle Joseph, another close person missing from his life. "Where is he?" Karl again wondered why they had not heard from him either. He must be dead, Karl was convinced. One worried thought led to another. He sighed deeply and started to think of all the work ahead of him the next day, not only did he need to work on the Major's desk but he had yet another Hitler Jugend meeting first thing in the morning. He really needed to get some sleep.

That's when he heard that loud knock on their front door. Sleep would never come. That was the cold, rainy October night the SS Albert and Ferdinand ripped him and his two brothers out of their home, against their will. He recalled Mutter crying and her trying to be strong while waving "Auf Wiedersehen," as they all were marched out the door. Her final pleading words to them were: "Stay together! Look out for each other!" Mutter was dealing with the nearly unbearable pain of losing her three sons in one night. She had then broken down sobbing, covering her wrinkled face with her weathered hands.

"Ade, Mutter! (Bye, Mother)" Hans and Karl both had responded one last time, while Ferdinand rolled Hermann out, who just lifted his hand up for a slight wave goodbye. And as fast as they had come that night, the SS soldiers slammed the big front oak door shut behind them. The house fell silent.

Hans tried to look back as they walked down the alley toward the idling SS truck, but Albert ordered them, "Geradeaus! Straight ahead, boys! Straight ahead!" And they had no other choice but to march toward the SS-marked Kuebelwagen parked outside awaiting them.

The cold rain was pounding the lifeless cobblestone.
Albert directed them to get into the back seat, first pushing each of their heads down. They quickly piled in, Hans slid over to make room for Karl.
They looked out the wet window, camouflaged in rain drops, and watched Ferdinand lift Hermann from his wheelchair into the back of his Kuebelcar parked in front of them. Hermann was very skinny, he needed to remain that way to be able to easily get around in his wheelchair, but Ferdinand's knees nearly buckled under his weight. The emotional pain was nearly unbearable, as they helplessly had to look on as their handicapped brother vanished in the car in front of them.
Albert then started the SS Wagon, pulled out and drove past Ferdinand's car. Both Hans and Karl turned their heads, trying to get one last glimpse of their brother. But it was too dark and rainy. All they could see was the rain-covered window. They reluctantly turned around and overwhelmed slumped back into the back seat of the wagon.
"Where are you taking us, Albert?" Hans reluctantly dared to ask, while looking ahead.
"Zum SS Hauptquartier! (to the SS Headquarters)" Albert snipped. "... And a last time, to both of you I am SS-Scharführer Albert Wuest! Don't call me by my first name ever again! That's an order!"
He got promoted. That was fast! Karl and Hans looked at each other, they knew how to read ranks and could easily imagine why Albert had moved up that quickly: Leading all the Spitzels (spies) in the

Hitler Jugend that helped turn people in who spoke up against the regime, was surely one of the qualities that helped him get there.

Karl knew where that grey-stoned, majestic 18th century building was located. He had walked by it many times, with its large sign "SS Hauptquartier" on the front and the many SS soldiers coming and going from there constantly.

The ride, over cobblestones only a few miles down the road toward the western outskirts of Nuernberg, was then quiet. Hans and Karl, both with their arms crossed in front of them, leaned back, exchanging glances here and there in the back seat. After a 10-minute ride, Albert parked on the side of the grey brick buildings, known as the SS barracks.

"Get out, we are heading to the central main SS building there," Albert ordered the two brothers, pointing toward the majestic building at the center of the SS barracks. It had two side wings, both surrounding a court yard.

Once inside, even though it was the middle of the night, soldiers and civilians were rushing around, as if everyone was in a big hurry to get someplace.

Albert handed over Hans and Karl to the first soldier he came across as they walked in.

"They are all yours; they are the Elheusch boys I mentioned. Get them registered." Albert saluted, clicked his heels and walked away in the opposite direction, not saying another word to either brother.

Karl couldn't believe they had played in the back yard with Albert just a few years ago. It couldn't be real that Albert, their former neighborhood friend, had just delivered them to the SS. They were living their worst nightmare. And Herman in a home? Karl couldn't stop worrying about that. What does that mean? What home?

"OK, follow me," the short, chubby SS-Rottenfuehrer (SS-Bandleader/corporal) with the name tag Schmidt ordered the boys, as he started waddling down a long hallway, expecting them to follow. He then stopped and pushed down the cast metal door handle to the first door leading to a large room, where a big-bellied SS corporal was sitting at a small desk right at the entrance.

"Sign in here," demanded the overweight SS soldier with the name tag Baecker. He handed each of them forms to fill out.

Karl and Hans wrote in the information requested on the form: Name, Address, Age, Birthdate, member of Hitler Jugend Y/N, Dad in the Wehrmacht (Army) Y/N, profession, and so on.

"Leave the blood type field empty. That's what we'll figure out here!"

The boys handed the filled-out forms back to Baecker.

"Now, find an empty station," he pointed into the general room area.

Hans and Karl stepped into the room and looked around at the large area, which was laid out to serve as a makeshift hospital room. There were tables and chairs set up with women in nursing gear, drawing blood from numerous boys dressed in Hitler Jugend uniforms.

"Sit down and get your blood drawn!" one of the SS soldiers commandeered Hans und Karl, as he pointed toward a few empty stations. They must have gathered all the boys from the neighborhood. Karl saw some familiar faces that looked up at him tiredly to give him a slight nod. He recognized Martin from his Hitler Jugend group, who barely acknowledged Karl, probably too upset about his fate.

Hans and Karl looked at each other, and then Hans asked the SS, "Why do they need to take our blood?"

"Just get it done, don't ask!" was his impatient response.

"They need to know your blood type in case you need a blood transfusion," Karl whispered to Hans.

Of course! It was finally sinking in: they were going to war. Karl had heard on Mutter's radio that Hitler was pulling in young and old, men and women under 60 and boys and girls as young as 12. With the Allied forces advancing, Hitler was desperate. So many lives had already been lost in this war, hundreds of thousands of casualties. There was hardly anyone left to fight his war, so Hitler was making his last attempt at winning it. Hans had heard on his mother's radio that the Allied forces already had invaded Italy, one of Germany's few allies, and they also already had liberated France. He knew that Germany was retreating on all fronts.

"Make a fist," said the boyish nurse, wearing brown, thick-brimmed glasses, and her eyes barely noticeable. She flashed a crooked tooth smile as she unbuttoned Karl's shirt sleeve, rolling it back for him, before he could get to it.

She tied a rubber band around his upper arm.

"You have nice veins. It's easy to get blood with these perfect veins," she said as she tapped on his right arm. She drew a slight smile from Karl. Then, without another warning, she surgically stuck in the needle. His watched his blood seep into the tube.

"*Eklig* (yuk!)!" said Karl, he was never too fond of blood, but before he knew it, he was done.

"Sit here and wait for the results," the nurse ordered him, then repeated the same procedure for Hans.

After they finished having their blood drawn, the large rectangular clock hanging from the center wall of the room showed 2 am. Exhaustion set in. Even the hard wooden benches looked inviting to sleep on, and nobody objected when they laid down and quickly fell asleep.

It seemed like he just had drifted off when the nurse was shaking Karl awake again. The morning's first daylight was streaming through the wide gothic windows into the make-shift hospital room, where hundreds of boys were strewn throughout, sleeping on the floors and on benches.

"Here are your results," she said in a soft and tired voice. She had been working all night. With a light touch of her hand on his shoulder, she handed him a piece of paper.

Karl was told he is just type "A," while Hans was type "A and ready for the tropics." Karl had heard, whether true or not, that Rommel took only type "A" soldiers to the desert in Africa because it was easier to exchange blood that way, but it had to be type "A ready for tropics." While the Rhesus factor had been discovered in 1937, it was not used yet to distinguish blood types.

Karl immediately remarked, “Hans, hopefully you don’t have to go to Africa while I have to stay here. I want us to stay together.”
“I think the war in Africa is lost!” Hans replied, but before Karl could respond, the nurse came back.

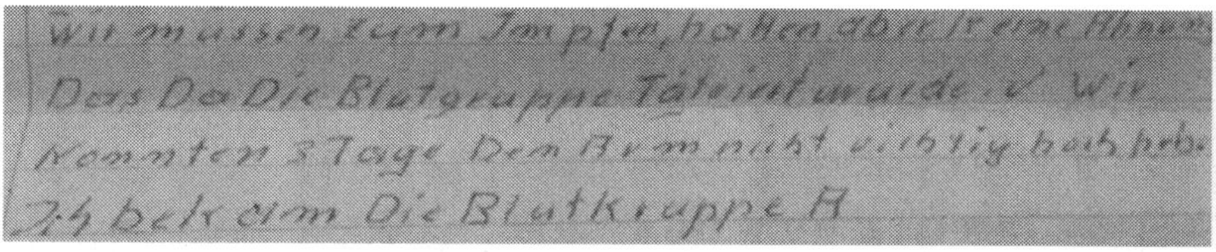
Wir mussen zum Impfen, hatten aber keine Ahnung Dass Da Die Blutgruppe Tätowiert wurde. & Wir konnten 3 Tage Den Arm nicht richtig heben. Ich bekam Die Blutkruppe A

“Now we’ll need to tattoo your blood type into your underarm near the armpit,” she ordered.

“A tattoo!?” Both boys’ mouths dropped open.

They noticed then that the other boys were getting ready to be tattooed. They had no choice. As the *Sanitäter* (medic) tattooed their underarms most boys remained stoic, gritting their teeth. They didn’t want to show weakness, even though it was one of the most painful areas to get a tattoo. The hypothermic needle stabbed over and over until that A was burned into their skin.

“Arghhhhhhhh!” few of the boys screamed out loud. Karl recognized one from his school before Karl had dropped out, to help out more with the carpentry. The boy’s name was Alois. He always had been one of the more studious kids in class. “*All that hard work apparently hadn’t paid off, and he now was also here being prepared for war, just like the rest of us*!”

Once they were tattooed, the corporal ordered them to line up in the largest hall located in the center of the compound, out the door right and straight down the hallway. They followed the directions but still they didn't really know what awaited them.

After the tattoo, Karl couldn't lift his arm for three days.

Chapter 6

War

Once tattooed, all 300 boys were handed nicely pressed field-gray SS uniforms and black leather belts along with SS jackets and black, shiny boots. They were ordered to change into the new attire right there. Karl and Hans could barely move their arms and a lot of moaning and groaning could be heard. The freshly tattooed underarm made it painful and slow to change into their shirts. Once dressed, they were ordered to pile their old clothes into a corner, from where they later they would be collected. Then they stood around waiting. What would their next orders be?

The teenage boys', 12 to 18 years old, were all huddled in the largest hall of the central main building in the cold SS compound. "*Where would we be fighting?*" Some were whispering thin speculations, but nobody wanted to draw attention. They knew that the Russians and Americans were advancing on both the Eastern and Western fronts, with massive air bombardments and ground movements against the German soldiers. A few were whispering about the latest news they had heard. They debated how much of a difference, if any, they could make at that point. Wasn't it too late to do anything? They were anxiously awaiting their fate.

The large double doors at the end of the hall swung open, and all heads turned in that direction. A *Hauptmann* (sergeant) with the name Mauer meticulously embroidered on his uniform stepped through the doorway, each side flanked on by a captain.

The Hauptmann, without looking left or right, marched straight up front toward the hall's prominent podium located at the front center stage. He was followed by the two Captains in cadence. The trio's sudden and seemingly rehearsed appearance underlined that something very important was about to take place.

The morning sun beams were streaming through the large stained-glass windows directly onto the podium, as if a spotlight was shining on the new arrival.

The boys' steady mumbling came to an immediate halt, and an anticipatory silence blanketed the room. All eyes were directed at the Hauptmann standing at the podium.

Hauptmann Mauer was a middle-aged, stocky man with red fat checks, blotchy skin and small, narrow set, dark eyes. Judging by his sizable belly and the enlarged capillaries on his oversized nose, drinking beer and Schnapps might have been one of his favorite pastimes. "*Drinking is one way to cope!*" Karl thought to himself. The Hauptmann's bloated head barely appeared a few inches above the podium, his body nearly swallowed whole behind it. The two young captains standing by his sides, towered over him.

"Heil Hitler!" Hauptmann Mauer shouted at the top of his lungs, sounding very angry. Then he swiftly saluted sternly with the common arm gesture, heels clicking, his fat arm stretched out above the lectern.

"Heil Hitler!" the boys immediately responded back in chorus along with the salute.

"Welcome!"

"You are here because we are counting on you! Hitler is counting on you! You are needed to help build the thousand-year Reich! It is an honor to be part of this endeavor! I am proud to be part of it!

He paused.

"Now, repeat after me!" Mauer ordered the boys, in a loud, commanding voice. "I swear to fight and defend my Vaterland until my death!"

The boys attempted to repeat the sentence; however, some spoke the words faster, while others just mumbled:

"I swear… I swear... to fight ... fight ... and defend my Vaterland until my death."

Their response was woefully out of sync.

Mauer's hands immediately grasped his hips and impatiently he screamed:

"Show me you mean it! Show me you are in for the fight of the thousand-year Reich until your death! Tell me you will fight for the thousand-year Reich! Louder! And uniformly this time! Especially you there!" He picked on one of the pimple-faced young recruits in the front row with the nametag Bach and pointed his fat finger at him. "Do your lips move?"

The red-faced young soldier, who immediately realized he was Mauer's target, quickly responded with a firm "Yes, sir!" with a salute and heels clicking.

"Yes, sir, what?!" Mauer demanded, his eyes piercing at the helpless boy.

"Yes, sir, I will fight for my Vaterland until my death! I will fight for the thousand-year Reich!" the recruit Bach responded firmly, emphasizing each word.

Karl pitied the fresh-faced boy, but at the same time was impressed by his firm response under that type of pressure. Karl himself tried to avoid any eye contact with the Hauptmann, mostly staring straight ahead and leaning over ever so slightly to hide behind one of the taller recruits in front of him. He surely didn't want to be made a spectacle of.

Hauptmann Mauer stepped back from the lectern, pausing, his arms folded behind his back. Everyone in the room continued to watch his every move, trying to read his face, wondering what would come next. Even Karl peeked up slightly at him. The Hauptmann again took a step forward toward the podium. His words bellowed through the hall:

"All now! Repeat after me this time, as loudly as you can and all together!

"I… swear... to... fight... and... defend... my... Vaterland... until… my... death!" Mauer emphasized every word in the sentence.

This time, the boys responded loud and in almost exact unison, adding emphasis to each word and moving their lips as much as they could:

"I will swear to fight and defend my Vaterland until my death!"

The sound of 300 young men shouting the coordinated response echoed inside and outside the large majestic SS hall.

Mauer nodded, barely noticeable, pressing his lips together. He was satisfied this time. Excited he responded: "Heil Hitler!" Again he gave the sharp salute with his stubby arm, and the boys mirrored his action.

Mauer announced: "You are now officially indoctrinated into the Jugend Panzer Division (youth tank division)!"

The boys kept their eyes on the Hauptmann, expecting to hear more. Some stood with their mouths wide open, not daring to look at each other, hoping to find more answers. What would come next?

Hauptmann Mauer glanced impatiently at the large clock hanging at the center of the white wall at the far end of the room, and continued in a lower voice:

"It is now 11:30. You have exactly 25 minutes to go to the *Kantine* (mess hall) and eat. This will be your last hot meal for a while. At 11:55 you will line up outside the main entrance. At 12:05 sharp you will board trucks that will take you to your destination. If you are not there, expect a severe punishment."

Mauer then paused and scanned the crowd, attempting to make eye contact with each of the boys. He lowered his voice so everyone had to strain their ears to hear:

"...Don't even think about trying to run. If you do, we will find you no matter where, I promise you. Not only will we track you down, we will also find your families."

Karl felt everyone inhaling and holding their breath. He knew threatening the boys with hunting down their families was one of the best ways to scare them into obedience. He felt his stomach sink. At that point, most everyone's father, brother, even grandfather or uncle was either still fighting or dead, and it was the women — mothers, sisters, aunts and grandmothers — who were left behind and the most vulnerable.

This threat assured that none of the young recruits would dare walk out any back door or try to escape any other way, perhaps on the way to their destination. They would do everything they could to keep their families safe.

Mauer repeated: "Be there at 12:05 sharp! You will form two lines. Hauptmann Bertrandt is in charge of all of you. Supporting him are SS-Scharführer Albert Wuest and SS-Scharführer Manuel Mueller. Follow their orders!"

He pointed at Hauptmann Bertrandt, another stubby soldier in his 40s, and at the two Scharführers Manuel and Albert, both thin and barely 18, standing proudly next to the lectern for their introduction. They energetically saluted Hauptmann Mauer, who in turn quickly saluted them back.

Heil Hitler! Heil, heil, heil!" Mauer rapidly ended his speech slowly moving his chubby arm back and forth with each "Heil."

The boys did their best to chime along. The halls echoed "Heil, heil, heil."

As swiftly as the Hauptmann had appeared, he disappeared out the large hall side door with his entourage. The doors slammed shut with a loud boom echoing in the hall.

Karl and Hans, along with the large group of freshly indoctrinated SS soldiers, turned to each other, the questions were flying. Within seconds, Albert put a stop to the slight mayhem and screamed:

"All to the mess hall now, *aber schnell!"* SS-Scharführer Albert pointed into the direction of the cafeteria. "We don't have much time! *Marsch, marsch!"* He continued to push everyone down the long hall.

One after the other they streamed into the hall. They lined up to grab bowls of steaming hot beef soup served from large aluminum pots sitting on the long tables along the stucco wall of the mess hall. All 300 recruits lined up, waiting to be fed. Karl doubted they all would get to eat before they had to be outside to pile onto the waiting trucks.

"Form two lines, one from the back and one from the front," ordered SS-Scharführer Albert. "Grab your plates and spoons here!" Albert pointed at the aluminum bowls, plates and spoons stacked neatly on a table at the entrance of the mess hall.

With large soup ladles, the enlisted soldiers rationed the soup to one soldier at a time, as fast as they could serve.

"Next!" "Next!" they said after each serving was splattered into the bowls. Further down a *Schütze* (private) scooped out potatoes using large ladles from two separate pots.

When it was finally their turn, Hans took both the soup and the potatoes. Karl, who was behind Hans, asked "What is that?" pointing at the steam rising from the pile resembling food on his brother's plate.

"Not sure. Potatoes, I think. I am so hungry I'll eat anything right now," Hans mumbled back.

"Move along!" the server barked.

Karl decided to have only the soup. "Soup please." And soup was poured into his bowl. He had always been the pickier eater.

"Karl, now is no time to be picky about potatoes. You need to eat anything they offer you," the ever-protective older brother Hans advised, as they looked for a place to sit. Karl just mumbled something and ignored his well-intentioned brother.

The brothers plopped down on the first empty seats next to each other on one of the crowded benches lined up parallel to the wooden dinner tables located throughout the mess hall. They ate as fast as they could. They were both so hungry, since it was the first meal they'd had since they were taken from home. Some of the soldiers were already starting to head toward the exit as others were still waiting in line to get their food.

"I wonder if they will have time to eat?" Karl nodded, with his head in the direction of quite a few of the waiting recruits.

Hans waved it away. "Nothing we can do about it. They are serving it as fast as they can."

Karl kept picking at his soup. "If this is our last warm meal for a while, I hate to see what the food will be like where we are going. There is hardly any beef in the soup. It's more flavored water than anything," Karl complained.

Hans gave Karl a questioning look. "You are really going to be this picky? Food won't be like Mutter's here; get used to it!"

Karl forced himself to eat the watery broth. His brother was right, this was no time to be selective, and there might not be another meal offered for a long time. How would they eat, wherever they are going? Food was already so scarce.

"Hurry up!" Karl said to Hans as his older brother shoved in his few last bites of that tasteless potato dish. Many more of the soldiers were now leaving the mess hall, while only a few remained in the food line. When Hans and Karl finally rushed out, many of the recruits were already lined up in the inside of the main exit. Everyone was anxious to get to where they were supposed to be going.

"Form two lines!" SS-Scharführer Albert ordered again, motioning with his outstretched arms at two parallel lines to his left and right. "Gefreiter Schenk! Tell everyone in the Kantine to come out now!" Albert screamed the order at a dark-haired soldier standing in the far back.

Hans and Karl looked at each other. Yes, some would go hungry on this new journey.

"The line to the right will go to Linz with me and the line to the left will go to Steg with Scharführer Mueller. *Schnell, schnell!* 150 men on each side! Count down, you start 1, 2..."

They were going to Austria! Karl had heard of the two cities in Austria located in the Alps very close to each other. He and Hans squeezed into the same line on the right to make sure they would end up going to Linz together. Not only were they making sure they were honoring one of Mutter's last requests to look out for each other, but

Hans naturally felt protective of his little brother. He promised himself he would make sure Karl did not ever have to be alone on this journey.

It was Karl's turn to count "130" and then Hans "131." The last few soldiers behind them, and all those who trailed in from the mess hall, finished up counting to 150 on each side. A few soldiers had to switch lines to make it an even 150. Each side was then told to exit through their respective doors, right or left.

Outside, soldiers who were part of the organized inductee effort directed the new recruits towards the connecting brick building from where each had to pick up their Maschinenpistolen 40 ("Machine pistols 40"). While they had learned to shoot rifles during many of their Hitler Jugend exercises, it was now time to learn how to use a machine gun. The trucks idling on the side of the cobblestone road were parked in a convoy ready to take them to their shooting range. They would have the afternoon to practice.

As many of the young soldiers as could fit, squeezed onto the cab of each of the trucks. Before the trucks took off, Albert and his counterparts checked off a list with the recruits' names and marked each name with their respective truck number. It was their way to keep inventory of all the soldiers-to-be.

The trucks then took them to the shooting range, where each recruit was taught how to use their machine guns, how to load them, aim and shoot. They were practicing on various targets setup in the distance. After a few hours of introductory training, they were herded back onto the trucks, to be transported to their final destination.

It was a bumpy but mostly quiet three-hour ride to Linz. They couldn't see outside. The young men were huddled together as they tried to keep each other warm on that cold October day. There was no heat in the back. Nobody talked. They were all too tired and cold, some still hungrier than others, and the realization had settled in that their fate was in the hands of the SS. Hans fell asleep to the continuous humming sound of the truck's diesel engine, rumbling down the country roads. Finally in deep slumber, his head fell over onto his little brother's shoulder. The last couple of days had been exhausting for all of them. Karl just looked across at the other soldiers sitting against the wall, his mind was wandering.

"How long will we be in Linz? What will we do there? There is no fighting front, at least not yet. Or is the enemy that close?" Karl had heard the Russians were closing in, but didn't think they were already in Linz.

The thoughts kept piling on, but after a while the exhaustion caught up with him, and Karl also fell asleep. His head nodded over on top of his brother's head, nestled snug on his shoulder.

"Wake up, we are here!" Karl woke to Alois, the soldier sitting on the right side of him, shaking his shoulder. Karl in turn nudged his brother who was still asleep: "We are here. We need to get off."

One by one, they jumped off the truck. The sun was setting already, and in less than 30 minutes it would be dark. Everyone lined up quickly with Albert already barking orders at them:

"We need to set up the tents! Grab the poles and tents over there! Then also take a spade from those trucks over there." Albert pointed toward two trucks parked on the side of a graveled road.

One of the young recruits eagerly ran toward the truck loaded with spades. "I'll hand the spades down," he excitedly volunteered on his way.

"*How can he have this much energy*?" Karl wondered in amazement. The soldier's name was Anton Walter, and he had sat next to Karl in the cafeteria. They had a brief introduction and small exchange discussing their blood types.

A gunshot echoed through the cold mountain air. Startled, Karl looked in the direction of the shot. Albert had fired his rifle in the air.

"Stop! You are not to do anything unless I order you to do so!" he angrily screamed at Anton. The baffled young SS stopped mid-run and reflexively covered his head.

"Get back in line!"

"Yes sir!" Anton responded, red-faced and shaken, he trotted back into the line.

"Schütze Milz there on the back of the truck will hand down the tent poles and the spades! Albert motioned to the soldier standing near the truck. "Now, one by one you all go over there and pick up your tools!" Albert continued his demands.

The young SS soldiers, some more eager to help out than others, each lined up to grab the equipment.

"First, set up the tents. Then start digging the trench along here," signaled Albert. "They each will need to be about 500 meters long, 2 meters wide and about 1.5 meters deep!"

Albert virtually marked the trenches, pointing with his rifle up and down and sideways: "1,000 meters along here should stop some of the tanks."

"*He shouldn't be swinging a loaded rifle like that,*" Karl was again very irritated by Albert.

Karl then scanned the brown grass fields covering wide open space until far in the distance; he saw the edge of a forest against the majestic Alps. The air was crisp and the sky had a pink hue from the setting sun. There was a light breeze. They were lucky there was no snow yet. Only the mountain caps were covered in snow. It had been a mild October so far.

Karl knew that since they were near Linz, they were very close to the Eastern border. Czechoslovakia was about three hours away from where the Russians were moving in.

They quickly set up their tents, then they were ordered to dig.

"Line up and start digging now!" screamed Albert.

"It's getting dark," Karl tried to protest.

"Stop complaining! You still have at least 20 minutes of daylight. Get going!"

"Auf, let's get started!" Hans mumbled, in a resigned tone to his brother.

"Yep, you'd better, and fast!" Albert seemed specifically interested in Karl and Hans' interactions and never missed a word, no matter how quietly they tried to communicate.

"We don't have much time!" Albert went on, seething at them. "The Russians are not that far away; they are closing in! This is just one of the many trenches we'll dig to stop them from getting any further! They will roll over my dead body, but I will not let a single tank get through under my watch! Get to work now, *aber schnell!"*

Karl and Hans, with their foldable spades in hand, walked over to line up next to the other soldiers who had already started digging on each side of the five-meter-wide space destined to become a trench. The wind was picking up, and Karl felt a chill despite his woolen jacket.

Stomping his boot on the spade, using all his strength and digging into the ground as hard as he could, Karl got to work. So did his brother, along with the rest of the soldiers.

Karl's first stomp only dug into the first layer of grass and some dirt. The ground was hard and didn't want to budge. Karl moved a couple steps to the side to find softer ground. He pushed the spade in again with his boot and dug a bit deeper. Karl decided to stand on the spade with both his boots, and putting his full weight onto it, he jumped up and down on the spade. Slowly, the dirt made way. Because of the recent milder temperatures, it was still possible to dig, but soon the ground would be entirely frozen and very difficult to work with. It became clear this digging would be a strenuous process.

Another few trucks of soldiers arrived. All 150 of the SS soldiers were lined up and working on digging the *Panzergraben* (tank trenches), though it was getting so dark they could hardly see.
"Time to wrap up! Keep your spades with you. They are part of you now, along with your machine guns!" Albert ordered. "You are responsible for them. If you lose them, you won't get them back, there are no replacements, and you will be stuck here without any tools or weapon!"
Their first day as indoctrinated SS came to an end. Tired and hungry, they fell asleep in their sturdy tents.
Early the next morning, the digging continued. One spade of dirt was heaped onto the next, arduous tedious digging continued, minute after minute, hour after hour. After the sun was nearly above them and what seemed forever of laboring away, Hans heard some of the soldiers near him complain. "I need a break," one said, and another, "I am thirsty!" They both sat down on the ground, laying their spades next to them.
Albert immediately marched over to them and ordered, "You get a break at noon; *mach weiter;* keep going! Get up!"
The soldiers responded with some grumbling and slowly got up to continue digging.
"Mensch, I am also thirsty," Karl whispered to Hans. "I wonder how much longer it is until noon." Neither had the luxury of having a watch.
Hans responded, keeping his voice down "Judging by the sun's location, it must be close to noon. 30 minutes or so?"

"I am not sure I can make it that long," Karl said, dehydrated and exhausted. Sweat was pooling on his forehead, and he wiped it with the back of his hand.

Both were feeling weak from eating so little in the past 48 hours. When Albert walked by to oversee the progress up and down the trench, Karl whispered so others couldn't hear:

"You should at least allow people to drink water! Everybody is thirsty. How often did you drink water and eat for free at our house?!"

That was the only reference Karl made to Albert about their common childhood memories since Albert's radicalized transformation. Growing up, Albert had spent more time at their house than at his own, because he loved Mutter's cooking.

Albert looked at Karl for a few seconds in apparent disbelief, as if pondering how to respond to Karl, who dared to bring up the past to him, the senior rank in charge. While keeping his eyes on Karl, Albert yelled an order at a soldier working 50 meters away:

"Grefreiter (Lance Corporal) Schenk! *Komm her!* (Come here)"

The soldier near the spade truck, who pretended not to have noticed the interaction, but had been watching it intensely all along, quickly marched toward Albert.

"Jawohl Herr SS-Scharführer?" he asked Albert eagerly, while saluting.

"Gefreiter Schenk, what time can you be ready to give everyone water?"

“Herr SS-Scharführer, I am ready now. I can take each of their water containers and fill it with water,” he gestured toward the water cisterns on the back of a truck. He had filled it with fresh water from the nearby creek that snaked through the mountains.

“All right, then, the soldiers here are thirsty and tired. Get them water now!” ordered Albert.

“Jawohl, Herr SS-Scharführer!” the lance corporal immediately saluted, half-grinning. He clicked his heels, turned around quickly and marched toward the water truck. He was ready to do his share to support the troops. In no time he returned with the containers filled with water.

“Hier!” he handed the water container to the first soldier in line.

“Trinke (drink) and pass it down!”

Lance Corporal Schenk then ran back and forth, handing back the containers asking everyone to pass them down.

Karl reached out his hand to signal he still didn’t have any water.

Only a few steps away, Albert stepped over and grabbed a container from the corporal and then marched back to Karl and handed it to Karl personally.

“Danke,” said Karl, grabbing it with a grateful look at Albert, and right after Karl gulped his first sips he gave the container to his older brother standing right next to him: “Hier, drinke!”

Parched Hans eagerly grabbed it and gulped it as if he had been stranded in a desert for days, drooling water down the side of his mouth. It was almost empty when he handed it back to Karl.

“Finish!” and Karl downed the rest.

"Ahhhh! Much better!" Schenk was right there, and grabbed the empty water container and replaced it with the full one in his other hand. "Hier!" he handed it to Karl.
"Vielen Dank, thanks." Karl very much appreciated the accommodating gesture from Lance Corporal Schenk, who didn't look much older than Karl. He's 18 at most, Karl thought to himself.
"What about you? Did you get anything to drink?" Karl offered the water back to the young corporal.
"I am good!" he waved the water away.
Albert stood there watching the entire back and forth.
"Back to work now, *Jungs* (boys)!" Albert ordered everyone, after all had their share of water.
Karl was slightly relieved at seeing this somewhat better side of Albert. He hadn't punished him for reminding him of their youth together. Appeased, Karl and Hans and the rest of the soldiers continued the arduous task of digging the trenches.
Hans was very close in guessing the time, as forty minutes later, at noon they were given a twenty minute break and were ordered to pick up their cooked but now cold potatoes, red apples, and one slice of bread each, along with some more water. The food was being rationed: it was supposed to be delivered by truck from "field kitchens" to all the locations where the different groups of soldiers were located, and it was supposed to be kept warm in thermos containers, but often the trucks arrived late or not at all and when they finally did get a new truck load of food, by the time it was fed to the young soldiers, it was almost always cold.

Someone mentioned not wanting to build a fire to heat it up because the smoke would have been visible for kilometers, giving away their location.

"How close is the enemy really?" Karl and everyone knew the Russians were closing in, but the question was how close? Nobody answered, though he knew it would not be long before the enemy was here. He finished eating his stale bread.

After the break they continued the digging until dark. Finally at 17:00 they were told to stop because it was nearly impossible to see. Exhausted, they all crawled into their crowded tents. At night it dropped down to -5 degrees Celsius. They were short on blankets, and Karl and Hans ended up sleeping with their winter coats and gloves on. This was the second of many freezing nights they would endure while here digging trenches.

The next morning, Albert woke them up by hitting large spoons at one of the tin pots. He was banging as loud as he could, taking too much pleasure in waking the workers in such a spiteful way. Then he ordered his young troop to stand in formation:

"We will also need guards for the area, day and night!" Albert bellowed at them.

"You will take turns! Two pair of guards at a time, each four hours! You'll take turns in alphabetical order and by age. We start with the oldest ones in this group first."

"Aachen, Acker, Almen, und Bach," he read the names off the list in his hand. "Step forward!"

The soldiers stepped forward: "Heil Hitler!"

All of a sudden, air raid sirens screeched from nearby Linz, loud enough to be heard many kilometers away.

"Air attack!" someone screamed.

Everyone frantically looked around, startled, not knowing what to do – there was nothing but wide open field; no building, no bunkers to hide in.

"Run to the trench!" Hans ordered his brother Karl. "Run!" as Hans dashed to the nearest trench. A few soldiers nearby started running with them toward the trench, some didn't move at all, frozen and overcome by fear.

Albert screamed, "Grab all your guns! All of you. We want to prepare to shoot at the planes if they fly over us!"

"Get your weapons!" Albert screamed at the soldiers nearest to him. "Then let's duck in the trench, but have the guns ready and pointed at whatever comes at us!"

Another group of five soldiers in the distance frantically readied the *Fliegerabwehrkanone,* the one single aircraft defense cannon the entire group had available to them. They rolled it into place, but then didn't know which direction to point it at. Nothing but blue horizon and white clouds could be seen in the skies.

The sirens kept blaring, its decibel levels moving up and down. Karl couldn't believe Albert was telling them to use their machine guns: Machine guns couldn't shoot down a plane. It would have to fly *really* low. Albert was never the smartest in class, but surely the Hitler Jugend or common sense would have taught him that.

“Everyone lie flat in the trench! Down!” Karl was screaming, instinct kicking in.

“You are not in charge!” Albert tried to shut down Karl, but realized he was out of ideas himself.

Karl attempted to out-scream the sirens blaring in the background. “We can’t defend ourselves, Albert!”

Then in an instant there was complete silence. Some soldiers who were still running stopped in their tracks. Everyone listened and mistrusted the eerie silence. Karl and Hans looked around in disbelief straining their eyes and ears to listen to the faintest sounds of planes, scanning the skies far into the distance.

Nothing!

A false alarm, maybe? They continued to scout the skies for a bit longer.

Karl broke the silence, getting up close for only Albert to hear: “Albert, we need a better plan to be better prepared for air attacks! What is everyone to do when we are attacked from above? We need a place to hide and can’t be out in the open like this!”

Albert barked back: “We only have one anti-air craft cannon for the entire group. We have machine guns and not nearly enough ammunition! Feldwebel Bertrandt has requested more ammunition, tanks, anti-aircraft support, everything for us! The soldiers on the fronts need more weapons to hold off the enemy. We are here to dig trenches. We are given spades. We don’t have enough equipment. We have only few machine guns! We have one air defense gun, we

have no rockets, and we have nothing! What is your plan, Karl? You are in this as much as I am. You tell me, what should we do?"
Albert got really close to Karl's face, his frustration pouring out, who in turn stared back at Albert in disbelief. At that moment, Karl felt he could read Albert's soul and recognized his resignation and feeling of helplessness. Albert was very scared!
"The enemy is now much closer, isn't he?" Hans, who was standing nearby, joined in, also realizing the Russians must be even closer than they had thought.
Albert just looked away and didn't respond.
"How close, Albert? How close?"
Albert looked down. Quietly and seemingly resigned, he responded, "I am not one hundred percent sure, but you are right, the Russians are very close. I think they might be within 100 kilometers or even closer."
Hans looked at Karl as if to say, can you believe this? He shrugged his shoulders and slightly shook his head.
Hans teased Albert, "..and you think those mole holes we are digging are going to keep the Russians away?"
They all knew the answer.
Albert still avoided eye contact with any of the brothers and kept looking down "The trenches will keep them away for at least a day or so. They will have to go around and find another way to get to Berlin. They are heading for Berlin."

“We have lost the war.” Hans turned to Karl, “It is practically over, with the Russians this close coming from the east and the Americans and other Allies coming from the west.”
“Let us not give up yet.” Albert sounded unconvincing. It was almost like the old days, when Albert, Hans and Karl were planning and scheming in their old neighborhood for things like how to quickly traverse the farmers forbidden large wheat field without getting lost. Forgotten for a moment was Albert’s rank in this SS troop. They were standing together, realizing that the war was nearly over. Germany had been defeated. Hitler had lied and continued to lie to the entire country. They had been led by a lunatic into this deadly, unwinnable war. How devastating this had been for their home country, as they had to helplessly watch it all unfold and now had been dragged into it against their will.
“Enough of that!” Albert jumped back, as if stung by a wasp. “I am in charge here!” He stormed toward the rest of the soldiers, scattered throughout the area in separate groups all puzzling about their fate after the false air raid alarm. What if planes had attacked?
Albert screamed as loud as possible for everyone to get back into formation. He didn’t address the sirens or what they should do when there is another imminent air raid. Instead, he continued his earlier orders. He had no solution. An air attack would be deadly for all the soldiers there out in the wide open space of the green grass fields, mapped against the alps.

"We need to guard the area of an 8-kilometer perimeter, two kilometers on each side. You are to cover the marked area for four hours, armed with your machine guns."

"What should we do when there is another air attack warning?" the pimple-faced soldier Bach piped up. Karl recognized him as the same soldier who was called out by Hauptmann Mauer, back at the SS HQ.

Albert squinted his eyes at the young SS. For a split second, he looked as if he were deciding what to do about this young soldier's disrespect and interruption mid-order. But then Albert surprisingly ignored the misbehavior and just continued, with even more irritation in his voice:

"When your guard time is up, after the four hours, switch off with the next four guards in line. We are setting up a roster." He repeated the names: "Aachen, Acker, Almen, Bach!"

"You two go this direction," he directed the young SS named Aachen and Acker to his right to go north, "and we will go east," he looked at the soldiers Almen and Bach, the young soldier who just had interrupted him. "We all will meet halfway!"

"Mark each kilometer as a *markstein* (milestone), so you know how far you have gone. Try to step out one meter at a time and count to 1,000 and then mark the one kilometer with a thick stick."

"Jawohl, SS-Scharführer!" was the response from the soldiers ordered on guard duty.

Albert turned around to direct his entire troop standing in formation:

"While I am gone, Gefreiter Schenk is in charge! You listen to his orders! Gefreiter Schenk knows to go to Feldwebel Betrandt if needed.

"...and one last thing: If there is another air raid warning, seek shelter in the trenches! Our machine guns won't stand a chance against the planes. It's best to just hide."

Karl and Hans looked at each other knowingly. Albert had actually paid attention to them and was trying to make sense after all. They all knew the end was near. What the end would look like and whether they would survive it were some of the questions they asked themselves each day.

"Auf, los! (let's go!)" Albert looked at his newly minted guards, and with that, they marched off toward the east, and the other pair marched north to meet halfway.

"Count 1, 2 ...," with each large step, each approximate meter, Corporal Bach measured the distance. After each 1,000 meters, Albert instructed them to mark the corners with a small tree branch. As they marched along, Albert started to sing the chant "Trust no Fox on his Green Heath and no Jew with our girls," which was a play on words based on the then famous Nazi children's book. Back home he had heard some SS claiming that Jews were taking their girl-friends away.

Nobody joined Albert in his idiotic rhyme, but Albert didn't seem to care as he continued to sing the racist song.

Back at camp, the soldiers continued digging the trenches. When night set Karl and Hans crawled into their tents, still wearing their winter coats to protect them from the chill. They huddled next to each other and quickly fell asleep during yet another uneventful night at camp, simply exhausted from the full day of hard labor.

It became their daily routine: continue digging the ravines. The ground got increasingly harder as the time went on and winter set in. It often snowed, and then there was no progress at all or it was slow at best. The days were short and much time was spent in the tents just passing the time playing the popular card game "Skat;" or writing letters on rare scraps of paper, that would never be sent; or talking and day-dreaming, while trying to stay warm. Morning, lunch, and dinner they were fed the same food: apples, cold potatoes, sometimes pears, but rarely any meat, never any warm food. They were told the food trucks were very delayed, even for the soldiers at the front. Surely they were running out of food.

"Will we starve to death?" Karl often wondered.

After two months in the field, Feldwebel Bertrandt informed them in a harsh tone that the front was closing in and that the German fighters were forced to retreat more and more. The front needed their help more than ever. He asked for volunteers, realizing how young some of these boys were. The front was now only 50 or so km away, they were told.

Albert handpicked the oldest soldiers from his troop. They didn't have any say in it. Hans, because he was already 18, was one of the soldiers told to join the fight at the front and immediately Karl volunteered also because he could not imagine letting his brother fight alone. Albert didn't object. He knew that if Hans went that Karl would insist on going also. “Anyone who volunteers to go to the front to fight won’t be denied the opportunity,” he mused.

They were transported 50 km East. When they finally got to the designated spot, they were handed heavy helmets and told to immediately dig in next to the soldiers who had already made their dugouts. They were told to duck and keep their heads down. This time, in order to protect them from view, the trenches were deep enough that they could almost stand in them.

As it got dark, they could see fire being exchanged in the near distance in the East. To Karl it looked like fireworks, but the Russians were still too far away for the German group to directly come under fire.

In the distance, Karl could hear the Russians soldiers singing and celebrating, because they knew the Germans were retreating and the Russians were winning the war.

Karl knew that the advancing Russians pilfered the German farmers’ wine kegs, beer, “most” (alcoholic apple cider), and other alcohol, and food; but their drunkenness and thievery was nothing compared to the other atrocities he heard about.

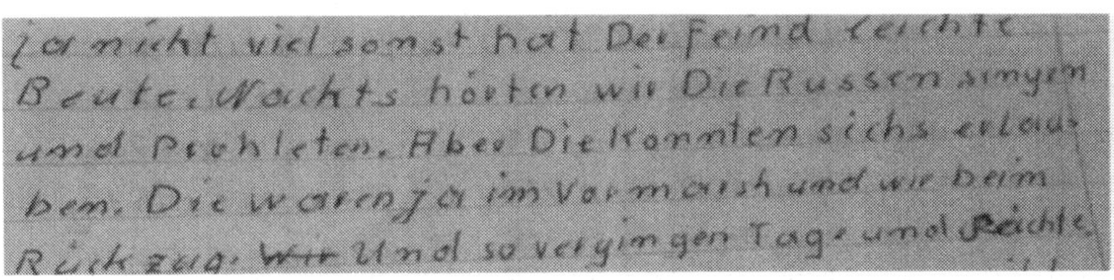
ja nicht viel sonst hat Der feind leichte
Beute. Nachts hörten wir Die Russen singen
und prahleten. Aber Die konnten sichs erlau-
ben. Die waren ja im Vormarsh und wir beim
Rückzug. ~~Wir~~ Und so vergingen Tage und Nächte.

That next day, in the very early daylight, during a hasty break from his dugout while trotting back from grabbing a few potatoes, Karl noticed a familiar-looking soldier passing by.

"Wait!" He reached for the soldiers arm to get his attention to look directly at him. "Aren't you?" The soldier now faced him, startled, and Karl recognized him immediately and his nametag confirmed: "Gefreiter Ferdinand! YOU! You came with Albert that night! You took my brother Hermann!"

Ferdinand's face lost all its color and he looked petrified. Karl was fuming, ready to leap at Ferdinand.

"Where is he? Where did you take him?"

"He is home!"

"What do you mean he is home?!" Karl leaned back ever so slightly as if hit by a punch. This was not a response he had expected. He frantically tried to read Ferdinand's green eyes to see whether he was telling the truth and the same time ready to attack him. They were out in the middle of nowhere at the front, soon to be shot at and highly likely killed, so Karl didn't really worry about what he would do to Ferdinand next and that was very clear to Ferdinand by Karl's demeanor. Ferdinand spoke fast:

"You have to believe me! Hermann is home! Albert wanted me to bring Hermann to a camp near Muenchen, it's called Dachau or something like that, and apparently a lot of cripples are sent there. But why drive two hours for a handicapped boy who can't do any work or support the fatherland in any way? I just don't have time for that! So once Albert and you all were out of sight, I just got

Hermann safely out of the car and wheeled him back into your house. It would have been such a waste of my time. I am here to support the war and win it, not do useless, busy work!"

Ferdinand now sounded matter of fact.

Karl was baffled. This was not the response he had expected and it still sounded unbelievable. An SS doesn't defy orders!

As if reading Karl's mind, Ferdinand quickly elaborated: "Albert should have never insisted we take anyone in a wheelchair, but I pretended to do it to appease him. I didn't want to disagree with him any longer. Albert has a terrible temper!"

"I know he does, but how can I believe that you took my brother back?!" As much as Karl wanted to, he didn't trust Ferdinand's story. Karl took a step closer towards the soldier who kidnapped his handicapped brother that night.

"I am telling the truth! I really brought your brother back home the same night, I swear!" Ferdinand seemed now really scared which was obvious to Karl. "*What is he still hiding?*"

Karl was still convinced that Ferdinand was lying and he decided to grill him further. Getting now very close to his face, he said: "I know Albert has a terrible temper. Aren't you worried you will get caught?"

"I knew Albert would leave the next day, he had orders to go to Linz to lead you guys the then newly minted SS group! I knew he wouldn't have had time to track down what happened to Hermann, he had bigger things to worry about and…," Ferdinand paused and lowered his voice: "…he trusts me!" He looked down, as if embarrassed that he misused that trust.

Ferdinand started to sound more convincing and Karl started to hope more and more that he was telling the truth, but remained skeptical.

"What did my Mom do when you brought him back that same night?" Karl squinted his eyes at Ferdinand.

"Your mom was ecstatic. She hugged me over and over and even insisted I take a handful of potatoes." Ferdinand smiled.

Handing out some of their potatoes was something Mutter would do. That was one of her trademarks, handing out potatoes or apples or other small food items at times to the kids who accompanied their customers, even though there often wasn't enough for them. But when questioned by Opa who was often irritated by that overly generous gesture, her response had been that they could always grow more potatoes.

"Don't ever let Albert find out! He will probably have me shipped off to that camp Dachau himself, if he does. The war is over soon and nobody will care anymore, but until then he just can't know!" Ferdinand now whispered, though no one was nearby.

Karl nodded. Of course he would not say anything to the brainwashed Albert. His anger at Albert was doubly renewed: How dare he order Hermann to a camp? What kind of camp would that be, anyhow? Hermann couldn't do any work. Albert will have to pay for this! Karl now felt like strangling Albert, maybe in his tent while he was asleep one night. But then Karl quickly dropped the thought for revenge. He wasn't a murderer.

At the same time, Karl wanted to scream, he wanted to really believe Ferdinand's tale about bringing his brother back home that same night they were taken in. Karl ran toward where he had last seen Hans holed up in the dugout.

"Hermann is supposedly at home with Mutter and Opa!"

"What do you mean, how do you know?" Could it be true? They wanted it to be true. Karl confirmed that initially he didn't believe Ferdinand either, but told Hans about Mutter offering potatoes as a reward, and that part of the story made sense and they started to believe it could be true. They wanted it to be true, they needed some happy news.

"Where is Gefreiter Ferdinand now?" Hans wanted to hear it from him directly and look him in the eyes. Was he really telling the truth? Or was he just appeasing Karl? A second opinion would be helpful here.

At that moment, firing erupted in the near distance. The shots seemed to be getting louder and closer. Using their foldable spades, rapidly they dug deeper and wider for better protection from direct gunfire, but they were still not safe from aircraft fire or hand grenades.

Their fear of dying needlessly for a war they didn't believe in grew larger by the hour. Karl prayed quietly, pleading with God. "Please let me get back home safe to my family. Please let them be alright."

"There is Ferdinand!" Karl saw him running towards their dugout.

A salvo of shots hit the group very close to them. Ferdinand was hit from behind. He fell down 10 feet in front of them. He died right there. Six other soldiers lost their lives that day.

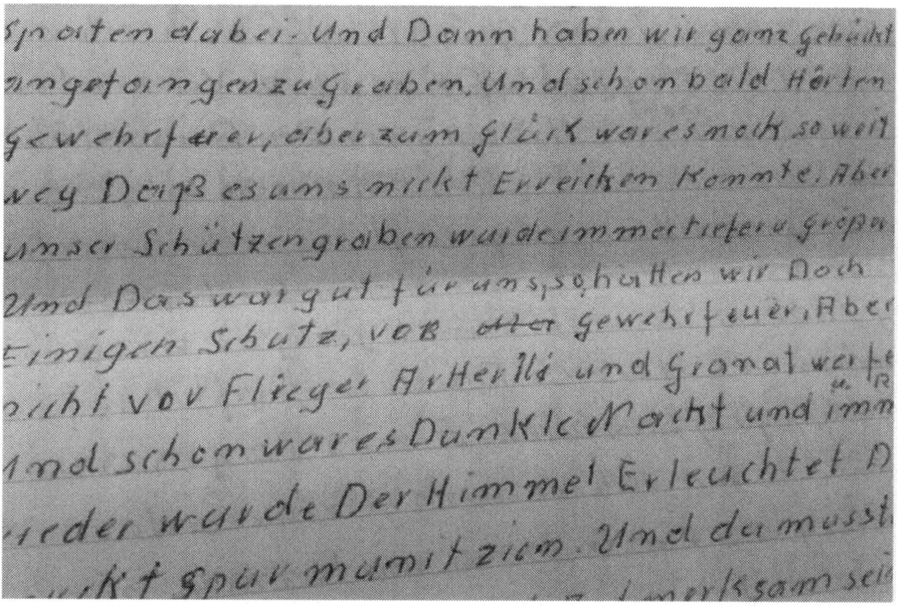
Spaten dabei. Und Dann haben wir ganz gebückt
angefangen zu graben. Und schon bald Hörten
Gewehrfeuer, aber zum glück war es nicht so weit
weg Daß es uns nicht Erreichen Konnte. Aber
unser Schützengraben wurde immer tiefer u. größer
Und Das war gut für uns, so hatten wir Doch
Einigen Schutz, vor ~~otter~~ Gewehrfeuer, Aber
nicht vor Flieger Artellerie und Granat werfe
und schon war es Dunkle Nacht und imm
wieder wurde Der Himmel Erleuchtet D
nicht spur munitzion. Und da musst

After the attack died down for a few hours, the ever so slight possibility of Hermann being back home improved their morale, but having to remain focused on yet another imminent attack was physically demanding and exhausting: over the next few days, they got little sleep, often sleeping while half standing, half kneeling. They never wanted to lie down completely, always having the machine gun propped up and ready. They were beyond fatigued, dirty and constantly hungry. Their food was rationed further: two potatoes in the morning, watery potato or sugar beet soup at lunch, stale bread for dinner and a few apples in between. They had no protection from the elements, wind, rain, and that evening it was even snowing. They were always cold, and the days of pure sunshine and calm were rare. A few of their fellow soldiers even suffered from frostbite.

As part of their daily nourishment, one day they were given unripe green apples, and that night many of the soldiers, including Karl and Hans, ended up with painful diarrhea. Having the runs was even more difficult to manage in the dark with no latrine nearby, while seeing "fireworks" that could kill them in the near distance. That night, Karl cursed his fate, the universe and swore off green apples forever.

Over a week had passed with them holed up in the front trenches, and another group of 30 soldiers who had retreated from further East joined them. All German troops were now in retreat, and this additional group that had joined them was now digging in near them. The new batch of soldiers was much older, and with one look at Albert's youngans, as they called them, Hauptmann Schwabe, who was in charge, refused to work with them: "I am not going to be responsible for these kids! Send them back to where they came from. My troop has this covered!"

What a great man! Schwabe completely disregarded Hitler's insane order that any – even young teenage boys - should be fighting at the front giving their lives. Someone said he had two sons their age, but that he hadn't heard from them in years. "Go back to dig trenches!" he insisted.

Without any complaints, Karl and Hans along with the rest of the youths in Albert's troop were trucked back 50 km and within a few days they were joined by the rest of the recruits they had parted with back in Nuernberg after they had been tattooed. Threehundred recruits were now digging within ten kilometers of Linz.

Karl would not have to volunteer for the front again, nor could Albert force Hans or any of them to go again. Karl was glad to be in a somewhat safer environment. But what would it mean to be in a safe environment these days? At least they weren't under direct attack but he knew that it would be only a matter of weeks or days before the Allied Forces would arrive there too.

The December nights and days became copies of themselves. It often snowed, they were always very cold. Karl would have missed Christmas completely if someone hadn't mentioned it. He had stopped keeping track of what day of the week it was. They were not allowed to officially celebrate this most important religious holiday. In silence, Karl and Hans prayed longer than ever. Karl reminisced about how before the war started, Uncle Joseph and Opa cut the Christmas pine tree for the house and set it up in the living room corner, tied by a rope to the wall; how Mutter and her boys decorated it with real clip-on, white wax candles and sparklers. The candles would be lit and reused every year until only stumps were left. How they sang *Silent Night* around the Christmas tree with the burning candles on it, until one Christmas the tree caught fire. Uncle Joseph had used blankets to distinguish the fire: a Christmas they would never forget for all the wrong reasons. That day in the war, especially, Karl was homesick. But no religious displays were allowed. Christmas came and went as just another day.

For months they continued the routine of laboring away at the ravines, they kept moving inland as one trench after the other was finished. They had dug acres and acres of trenches. It was March, some of the field flowers were starting to bloom: crocuses, daffodils and forget-me-nots were seen in the distance. One of Mutter's favorite flower was the forget-me-not. She was growing them in her garden and they bloomed in the spring and fall.

One day during their routine digging, Karl heard laughter nearby that got louder and louder. He paused to look up and figure out what the ruckus was about: Some of the laughing soldiers were pointing at two guards walking back toward camp, returning from their guard duty.

The young guards Bach and Milz were without their machine guns. Karl had seen them leave with their weapons; they were almost dragging the rifles on the ground being the youngest and nearly shortest in the group. But they were returning without their machine guns, and their pants were cut off.

Einmal wurde (auch) eine Stellung von Den Rüssen über-
fallen. Dann haben Sie Den Kameraden Die
Hosen (ab) ägeschnitten und gesagt Sie sollen nach
Hause gehen, Mit Kinder wollen Sie keinen
Krieg fähren. Ja und Dann ging es wieder
Rückwärts in Österreich. Die Ortschaft hieß

Karl put his spade down and walked toward the crowd of soldiers that now surrounded the young boys.
“What happened? Who did that to you?” Albert came storming toward the two boys at the center of the nosy crowd. He inspected them as if to make sure they were not hurt.
Bach responded with tears of frustration streaming down his dirty face: “The Russians!” pointing to where they came from, and then just looked down in embarrassment. Everyone looked east in the direction Bach was pointing, but there was nothing to be seen but flowered fields up until the forest tree line in the far distance.
Milz joined in and explained: “We walked just a bit past the four-kilometer marker. I know we shouldn’t have, but we wanted to find mushrooms in the forest. Pfifferlinge are my favorite, and I figured we’d find many inside the forest.
Albert interrupted him angrily. “Pfifferlinge won’t grow until late summer!” He, Karl, Hans, and the neighborhood boy Michael often went to collect those mushrooms in their nearby woods. Steinpilze was their favorite. They would sometimes spend hours in the forest searching for them. The excellent taste of fried Pfifferlinge and Steinpilze scrambled with eggs was the delicious reward.
Milz continued, “Are you sure?” For a minute he was sidetracked on whether his favorite mushroom was in season yet. But then he continued. “After a few steps inside the forest, out of nowhere two Russian soldiers appeared. I could not tell their rank. They are in their 30s. They tried to talk to us, but we don’t speak Russian and they don’t speak German. I froze. I couldn’t even use the rifle, it was

so fast. They pointed their machine guns at us. They pushed us to get down and one took out his knife, I thought he wanted to kill us. I thought this is the end. I was looking up in the sky just waiting for them to cut my throat." Milz also started crying. He was just a young boy.

Bach continued: "Then they just cut and ripped off our pant legs. Nothing else. They were trying to tell us something, they were signaling, I think to tell everyone here that the Russians won't fight with kids. I could understand him say 'Kinder,' and he waved his hands in disgust, and that's the only German word I understood. Then they yanked our rifles from us and marched away with them. And we ran back as fast as we could."

"How far deep in the forest were you? Are you saying they are right there in the forest line passed the fields?" asked Albert in a panicked voice. He pointed at the tree lining just a few kilometers downhill.

"Yes!" Bach and Milz agreed in unison.

"Do they know we are here? Were you being followed?" Albert continued the inquiry.

"I don't think so. I don't really know. No, they didn't follow us, we kept looking back, but they didn't follow us, they walked back in the forest laughing."

"Of course they can see us! We are sitting ducks!" Karl was being realistic.

Albert turned as white as Karl had ever seen him. Albert immediately jumped back and gave the order:

"Let's march further inland. We have to retreat towards the West."

With no objections, they packed up their tents, loaded everything on the trucks, and started marching inland.

After one hour marching, they arrived on the opposite side of Linz and quickly again unloaded. Albert ordered again: "Get back to digging the trench! The Russians are closer than we think. We won't let them get through here!"

Everyone looked at each other, mumbling and getting back into their digging positions.

"The Russians are here; it's just a matter of days!" Hans stated the obvious.

"We have lost the war. It is over. Why are we still doing this?" Karl asked, incredulous. Hans just shrugged his shoulder, defeated. "I guess it's not over until Hitler officially surrenders or he is killed! Why can't someone just kill that bastard?" They both could not stand to wait any longer for this to be over!

Nobody heard from or saw those Russians again. The guards were instructed to stick to the newly outlined 8-kilometer perimeter and stay far away from any tree line. Were those two Russian scouts just by themselves, far away from their troop or battalion? They must have been. They appeased themselves by thinking it must have been a fluke.

Feldwebel Bertrandt's troops had been digging at the ravines at one location or another for nearly five months, and it was again Hans and Karl's turn at four-hour guard duty, starting at midnight. As part of the routine, the two guards before them would wake up Karl and Hans when they had completed their shift. The brothers went to sleep knowing midnight would be here before they knew it. Exhausted, it took them only minutes to fall asleep.

When Karl woke up, he saw the sun making its way up on the horizon in all sorts of pink and red hues behind the Alps. Why had the guards not woken them up? Why didn't they come so they could relieve them? It was way past midnight – it was early morning! Karl stepped outside his tent and looked around: he didn't see any movement. All soldiers seemed to be in their tents asleep. He walked over to the tent next door and saw the other pair of guards that was supposed to take over with them at midnight still asleep also. Karl went back and woke his brother. "Hans, they didn't come and get us!" Hans rolled over and went back to sleep. Karl marched over to Albert's tent, one of the few larger tents set up for the higher ranking SSs.

Leaning toward the entrance of the tent, Karl tried to whisper as loud as he could without waking the others: "Albert!" Immediately he heard rustling in the tent.

"What?!" Albert stormed to the front of the tent, and ripped it open; angry at the disturbance.

"The guards didn't come to get us. They were supposed to come back and get Hans and me at midnight, so we could switch off." Karl whispered.

"Scheisse! Shit! They probably deserted us! Let's go look for them, I'll be right back." Albert went back inside the tent to put on his tattered coat and grab his machine gun.

"Let's get Hans, too," Karl offered. "Hans can come with us. I also have to get my machine gun."

They both walked over toward the tent where Hans was still asleep.

"Hans, wake up," Karl tried again to wake up his brother, whispering loudly, shaking his shoulder. "Hans, the guards didn't come to get us, Albert and I are going to look for them."

Hans opened his eyes. "What?"

"The guards are missing!" Karl repeated.

Hans jumped up: "What?"

"We are going to find them." Albert repeated.

"Come with us!" Karl directed Hans.

As he jumped up, Hans grabbed his coat, which had covered him, and he put it on while chasing Karl and Albert, who were already heading east. As he caught up, Hans noticed Albert and Karl were carrying their machine guns. Hans now remembered, "I forgot mine"

Karl just responded: "I've got you covered."

With that, the three continued to march east along the 8-kilometer marked-off perimeter. At nearly 300 meter altitude, this early in the morning, the winds were howling and blowing dust into their already cold faces. Though the sunrise was beautiful, covering the entire sky in a bright pink hue, they were walking directly into the rising sun and had to squint to see ahead of them.

They passed the two-kilometer marker with no sight of the guards. When they got to the four-kilometer mark, Hans pointed into the distance, where a bunch of vultures were circling.

"Look!" Hans started running. Karl and Albert followed suit.

In the distance, a few flecks of grey and brown could be seen in one of the few pockets of snow plotted throughout the landscape. They couldn't see exactly what it was as they ran directly toward the bright morning sunlight. They were fighting the wind.

Karl screamed in disbelief: "Is that them? *Mein Gott!"*

They got to the spot and found the four bodies scattered on the ground. Their throats had been slit, dried up blood covered their faces and necks.

"Mein Gott!" Karl was aghast. The gruesome scene nearly put them in shock. This was only their second time witnessing war casualties and it was just as disturbing as the first when Ferdinand was shot in front of them. Albert immediately ripped his rifle off his shoulder, aiming it, moving around 360 degrees, searching for the enemy, ready to shoot. There was nobody else to be seen, nothing but empty grass fields with the wind drowning out any other noise. Frantically they all scanned the far distant forest line. Beyond that, it was just acres and acres of deep, thick forest. The enemy must have been hiding in there. Anyone could be hiding behind the thickness of those tall black pine trees. They were probably being monitored as they stood there.

"Let's run back! Let's warn everyone and get backup," Albert started running back toward their camp.

"Wait – shouldn't we do something with the bodies?" Hans responded.

Karl agreed: "We should bury them."

“They are dead. Do you want to be next? I’ll have backup come for them!” Albert responded while continuing to run back to their camp. Without any more hesitation, Hans and Karl raced right behind Albert. The enemy could appear from the far away tree-line at any second. As they ran, they once in a while looked back in the direction of the bodies to see if anyone would appear: but nothing, still nothing but empty eeriness and the few vultures again circling.

Chapter 7

Americans

After the trio stumbled upon the murdered guards, they raced back to their base. Albert frantically notified Feldwebel Bertrandt, who, in turn, ordered a few of the older soldiers to go back to find the bodies, so they could bury them.

To prevent other guards from being murdered, Feldwebel Bertrandt ordered everyone to go in groups of four guards each now instead of just two, each armed with their machine guns. They were held responsible for keeping each other awake during guard duty, which was now a simple task given they all knew the dire consequences of falling asleep. Since Albert thought the enemy was easier on the youngest ones, also mostly the youngsters were sent. They suspected that the two guards had fallen asleep, making them easy prey. But they never were able to recreate the details of what exactly happened.

Within a few weeks, Karl seemed to have moved on from the shock of seeing his peers with their throats cut. But Hans still had night-terrors. Karl then often had to shake his brother awake in the dead of the night when he heard him moaning while tossing and turning. It took a lot of effort to make Hans realize he was just having a really bad dream.

Karl got more and more discouraged. He was convinced this was all such a waste of time; he didn’t see the point of having the guards at all. This entire effort was just a charade to give everyone in their little group the feeling of having some type of control. What were they to do if they were attacked? The enemy was close. Karl shrugged his shoulder at the thought of it, knowing how woefully untrained and unprepared they were in the face of any type of enemy attack. He knew it was just a matter of days, if not hours, before all of this was over. Would he and Hans survive this? A war they didn't believe in; they were prisoners of their own country.

The days were blending together. On May 8th, 1945, yet another cold early morning in the mountains, they were again shoveling dirt pile after dirt pile on top of another, time wasting away with them laboring at the trenches. The digging was much easier with the ground fully thawed. The cold winter days, when they didn't make any progress digging at all, were long behind them. Then they were making progress again, and it gave them a bit more purpose. Regardless, they were all constantly exhausted, cold and hungry. They had been here about seven months now, covering acres and acres of dirt, the group had dug a multitude of trenches, like gigantic moles had been at it, busy digging for years. The muscles in their backs were now constantly aching; their faces were completely weathered and burned from the relentless wind and cold. Whenever a trench was completed to Albert's satisfaction, trench by trench, ditch by ditch, they moved further inland, away from the Eastern front, from where the enemy was rapidly closing in.

The deep trenches surely would slow the enemy down, or wouldn't they? Karl was still not convinced. He straightened his sore back and held it up with one hand, as he watched his breath float in the clear, cold mountain air. He didn't know what day of the week it was. He and the other soldiers had already been shoveling since the crack of dawn. He was thinking about lunch. His stomach felt empty;

constant hunger pain was part of the daily routine. The last thing he had eaten was a cold potato the night before, along with some cold water he fetched from a creek nearby. They had found some sugar beets, but they tasted horrible raw. He felt weak.

Gripping the spade with his dirty and calloused hands, he continued the repetitive monotonous task, relentlessly stomping down onto the beat-up tool and then throwing the dirt up on the pile, again and again. As the trench got deeper and wider, the dirt piles got higher and higher. His muscles had grown over the last months, but also his arms and legs were sore from the daily labor, and he felt dirt everywhere: under his fingernails was a pile of crud, and his face was dirty. His uniform clearly needed another wash, he couldn't remember the last time he washed it. He kept dreaming about a hot bath in his home, a bath he would soak in until the water got cold. Mutter would fire up the wood stove to get the bathwater to a boil, and one after the other, Mutter, Opa, Karl, or Hermann each would refill the tub for their turn until all the hot water would be gone. The next person in line for a soak would have to add the wood logs to the fire and wait another thirty minutes before being able to take a hot bath. They would continuously have to feed the wood stove to heat the bathwater until everyone was bathed.

Karl continued to daydream, standing knee-deep in the ravine he had helped dig, when out of the side of his eye he caught a movement. He looked over and recognized someone running in the far distance down the grassy knoll toward them. Karl strained to hear. The screaming was muffled, the runner too far away for Karl to make out who it was and what he was saying. Karl stopped shoveling, with one last hard step on the spade it dug in standing up. He quickly took a few steps east in the direction of the runner. Squinting against the morning sun, Karl strained his eyes and finally recognized his comrade Anton closing in on the distance while still running and screaming. Finally Karl could also make out the words:

"Der Krieg ist vorbei! (The war is over!)" Anton kept running toward them and repeating:

"Der Krieg ist vorbei!"

"Der Krieg ist vorbei!"

Karl couldn't believe what he was hearing. "What?" Karl heard exactly what Anton was screaming, but he had to ask again. He just couldn't comprehend it — he was getting goose bumps, and it seemed the wind was chillier than before. For a second, he almost felt paralyzed. His thoughts were summersaulting. Others with their dirty faces and dirty clothes now crawled out of their ditches as if in slow motion. None of them could believe what they were hearing. All gaped eagerly in the direction of Anton, who was still running toward them. Karl sprinted toward Anton because he needed to hear it again.

Anton was waving his hands and continued screaming *"Der Krieg is vorbei"* over and over, now stumbling over his own feet in the dried cold dirt while running toward them.

Karl caught up with Anton, who was trying to hoist himself up on his knees, hardly able to catch his breath. He must have been running for a while, and without much to eat in the past months, any such physical exertion took a major toll on the body. Karl grabbed Anton by his shoulders, propped him up with both hands and tried to look him into the eyes. "What?" Karl repeated. "How do you know?" Anton stared through Karl: "I heard it — the war is over. Hitler killed himself!" Anton's chest was heaving and breathing hard with each word. Excitement covered his muddy face while the smile lines around his hollowed eyes crinkled. "Can you believe it?! The war is over?" His crooked teeth were widely exposed, against his dirty face. "What? Hitler killed himself? Who told you?" Karl pounded him with questions and continued to prop him up by his shoulders. "Feldwebel (Staff Sergeant) Bertrandt told me." Anton's smile got smaller as if he were a bit annoyed at Karl for doubting him. Anton's breathing slowed down, and he turned around to point at the Feldwebel, whom they then could see in the distance staggering down the hill as fast as his stubby, 40-year-old body let him. Anton and the Feldwebel had been on a scouting mission, they wanted to see how far the enemy fire was. They knew it was coming closer because they could see the fire at night. There they ran into German soldiers who had heard it on their *pfanzersende-* und *empfangsgeraet* (hand-held transmitters and receiver).

The group of "trench" soldiers now surrounded Karl and Anton, all eager to hear the latest information.

"What? Hitler killed himself?"

Nobody seemed to really grasp what they were hearing; Hitler, so indestructible, killed himself? He didn't give anyone the satisfaction to allow them to kill him; no, he had to kill himself and take away that privilege from anyone. His last hurrah.

After all this time, the war was finally over. After all their family hardships, being ripped from under their mother's arms, Hermann being taken — did Ferdinand really bring him back home? — his missing Uncle Joseph! Every soldier here had a similar story of missing brothers, fathers, cousins or uncles, most missing in action.

"Nooooooooo!!!?????!!" Schuetze Milz cried, and his cry echoed in the cold mountain air.

The questions were flying:

"What does it mean?"

"Can we go home?"

"How do we get home?"

"Who will take us home?"

"Will the Russians take over?" "The French? The Americans?"

Nobody had any answers.

"Will we become prisoners?"

"They will kill us!"

"If the Russians take us prisoners they will kill us!" confirmed Anton "I have heard they have orders to not take any prisoners."

"Anyone can take us as prisoners, the Americans, the French, the English; just not the Russians," responded another soldier.

The uncertainty swiftly turned into panic.

Schuetze Bach and Walter made a pact with each other not to surrender to the Russians:

“Anyone but the Russians! I would rather kill myself than have the Russians capture me!” They had heard the horror stories of the Russian soldiers’ brutalities; soldiers being killed on the spot, torture, stories of burning houses, rape of grandmothers and even children.

Some of the young trench diggers were visibly shaking, rubbing their arms, arms crossed, teeth chattering, partially due to the cold air but mostly as a reaction to the news. They were not really soldiers; they were kids who had hardly fought in battle. They had only dug trenches. But would the Russians believe them? Would the Americans care? Some of the boys were pacing back and forth, looking down trying to find a solution, some looking at Karl for answers.

Karl motioned with the palms of his hands up and down to tell everyone, *“langsam gehen* (slow down).” Karl saw that Hans’s face had lost all its color.

Feldwebel Bertrandt finally got to the group and instructed in a resigned tone: “Hitler is dead! We have to surrender to the Russians. They are about five kilometers that way,” he pointed back to where he came from “If we surrender, they will have to treat us as prisoners of war.”

“I am not waiting around for them. I am not going to be tortured by them,” the pimple-faced Bach said, and in panic he started running west as fast as he could. Walter and other soldiers immediately darted after him.

For a split-second Karl thought about joining them, but quickly changed his mind because he didn't want to be a deserter, and there was really no place to hide. The Allies would catch up with them one way or another. No one knew what they could expect further inland. Karl was still watching the soldiers dart away toward the west when he heard a scream:

"No – don't!" Karl looked over and caught Bertrand leaping at Schuetze Milz, who had snatched Feldwebel Bertrand's Mauser HSc handgun and now held it against his own temple. "I'll never surrender!" with that a gunshot echoed through the gloom mountain side.

"Noooo!" Karl tried to stop the suicide, but Schuetze Milz had already pulled the trigger. "Nooooo!" Karl and Bertrand and Anton tried to catch Schuetze Milz's fall, and Anton was holding him up in his arms. Blood was streaming down the right side of Schuetze Milz's face, leaking onto Anton's uniform.

"Schuetze Milz, no, no, no." Anton whimpered, trying to hug the limp body. Schuetze Milz had always been there for everyone, and they had become close the last few months here together. A few times, when Karl complained of hunger, Schuetze Milz had even shared his potatoes with Karl, ignoring his own hunger.

Another shot echoed in the quiet cold air, and then another. They couldn't keep up with the mayhem that had broken out. Gefreiter Schenk shot himself. Schuetze Milz and Gefreiter Schenk were close friends, and Karl and Hans had also gotten close to them.

Another shot was fired; Martin shot himself, and it was followed by another shot!

This time it was Feldwebel Bertrandt shooting his rifle in the air, screaming “Stop it! I order you all to stop it!”

Frantically, he tried to control the pandemonium that had broken out as soldiers feared they would become prisoners of war and be tortured.

“Put down your weapons! We have to surrender!” ordered Feldwebel Bertrandt

“Why can’t we try to defend ourselves? We have machine guns!” Albert was desperate.

“We are outnumbered by the thousands – there is no use – it would be suicide trying to defend yourself here, you will have us all killed”

“Put down your weapons!” the Feldwebel repeated the order this time, sounding more impatient. “Collect them here in a pile, so the Russians can see them openly.”

Bertrandt then put his weapons down onto the ground, Karl and Hans followed. The soldiers then, one after the other, hoisted the weapons off their shoulders and piled them on top of each other in the grassy field.

“The Russians will want us, the older SS,” Feldwebel Bertrandt stated, as he tried to appease the younger soldiers.

Albert came to Feldwebel Bertrandt’s support addressing the panicked group: “You all are mostly too young. They will leave you alone.” He looked down solemnly, because he knew what that meant for him.

Karl chimed in agreement. "Yes, we had nothing to do with this. We were forced into this. I don't consider myself SS and never have." There he said it, for the first time he spoke publicly about what he had felt all along. No he was not an SS; no he did not believe or had ever believed in the Nazi ideology. Bertrandt and Albert just looked at Karl, not too surprised – and at this point nobody cared enough to respond.

The Allied soldiers by then knew that SS could be identified by their blood type tattoo. Karl heard of a friend who was treated in a SS hospital, and like Karl he was tattooed, even though that guy wasn't Waffen-SS. Yet the Russians wouldn't care how willingly they joined the SS or how they got the tattoo. Given the language barrier, they wouldn't be able to communicate with each other, since nobody spoke Russian and worse, nobody would even take the time to listen to this explanation.

An older SS, Unterscharfuehrer Schmidt, was approaching Karl with a razorblade between his beefy fingers.

"*What does he want*?" was all Karl could think for a split second. This Schmidt guy's demeanor had always made him feel uncomfortable; there was something odd about him that Karl couldn't figure out. Leaning in uncomfortably close against Karl's chest, Schmidt now stuck the razor blade in Karl's face and half-whispered the order, "Here cut it out!" lifting up his arm and rolling up his sleeves while nodding at his SS blood-type tattoo on his underarm.

"What?" Karl asked in disbelief.

“Cut out the tattoo! They are going to kill me if they see it.” Schmidt begged.

“But they will see the fresh wound right there. They can easily figure this out.” Karl countered.

“I can tell them I got in an accident, I can make something up.” The SS Unterscharfuehrer was pleading desperately, even though the request was utterly ridiculous to Karl; anyone could figure out the source of that wound.

“Just cut it out!” Schmidt gritted his teeth, pleading.

“The tattoo is really deep, I will have to cut out a lot.”

“Just cut it!” Schmidt intimidated Karl by now pointing the razor blade right under his throat.

Karl grabbed it from Schmidt, and frustrated, started puncturing the Unterscharfuehrer’s skin covering the flabby underarm. Blood started pouring out immediately. The tattoo was very deep: four to five millimeters deep. Karl stopped and turned away disgusted, with his hand covering his face: “I can’t do this.”

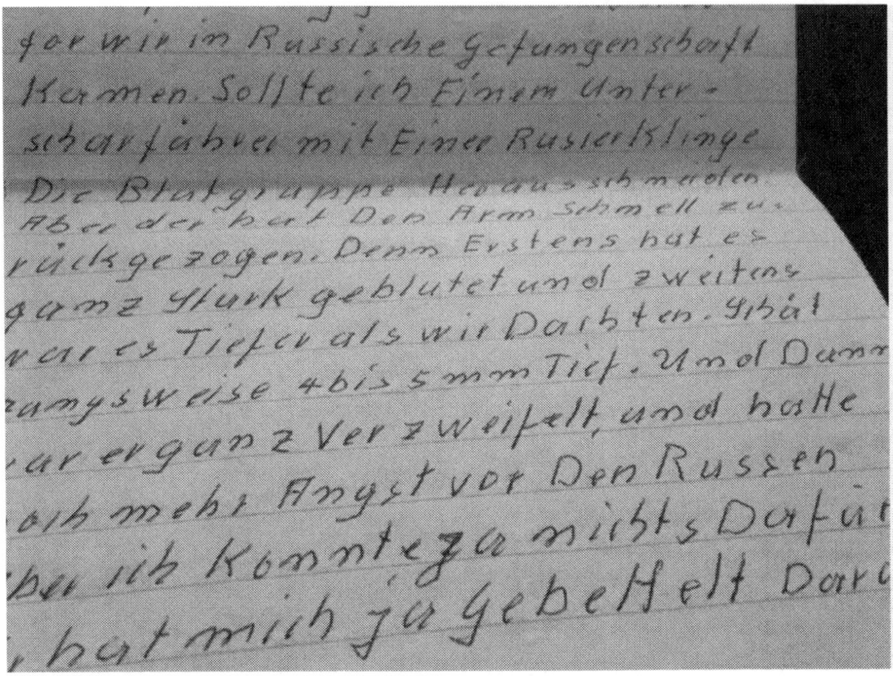

for wir in Russische Gefangenschaft
Kamen. Sollte ich Einem Unter-
scharführer mit Einer Rasierklinge
Die Blutgruppe Heraus schneiden
Aber der hat Den Arm Schnell zu-
rückgezogen. Denn Erstens hat es
ganz Stark geblutet und zweitens
war es Tiefer als wir Dachten. Schät
zungsweise 4 bis 5 mm Tief. Und Dann
war er ganz Verzweifelt und hatte
och mehr Angst vor Den Russen
ber ich Konnte ja nichts Dafür
hat mich ja gebettelt Dar

Schmidt impatiently ripped the razor blade back from Karl, tearing the skin on Karl’s thumb.

“Ouch!” Karl licked the drops of blood off his injured thumb.

Schmidt now kept cutting at his own tattoo, as he bit his lips and let out a continuous growl to suppress the pain. The tattoo was much deeper than expected. There was no way he could cut it all out, without leaving a deep gash, but Schmidt kept cutting.

Before Karl could run to try to get some cloth to wrap around the SS Unterscharfuehrer’s arm, they were startled by the noise of a squeaky motor. Within a few minutes they could see in the distance the Russian tanks rolling down the same grassy knoll that Anton had just come from. The tanks rolled up and down through the trenches they had dug with ease. Nothing could stop those monstrosities. Seven months of digging in vain!

“Russians!” Another batch even closer than they thought.

Gmunden-Griesskirchen, Eines Tages am 8. Mai Hörten wir von anderen Kameraden das Der Krieg aus war. Und wir kamen mit anderen Soldaten zusammen. es wurden immer mehr, und auf Einmal Kamen Russen mit LKW und Panzern wir wurden zusammen-getrieben. Mussten uns Aufstellen in Reihen Dann Hies er Oberkörper frei Linken Arm Hoch. Dann mussten Die mit der Blutgruppe auf Die Linke Seite Das waren SS die verhassten

“All, get ready to surrender!” ordered Feldwebel Bertrandt calmly. “Put your hands up, everyone! Show them you are giving up!” the Feldwebel ordered the remaining kid soldiers. “Otherwise, they will shoot you.”

Feldwebel Bertrandt had wrapped a white cloth around the end of his machine gun and as a sign of surrender held it up with one hand, along with his other hand high up in the air. He bravely stepped into the direction of the convoy that was heading toward them.

One after the other, the boys lined up side by side with their hands up, anxiously awaiting their fate.

The three tanks squealed toward them with at least 50 soldiers marching next to each side of the tanks, pointing their guns at them. The tanks came to a stop in front of the ridiculously young, dirty and skinny German soldiers, each of whom held their hands high in surrender. What must the Russians have been thinking: fighting a war with kids? Some of them probably had sons their same age waiting at home for them to return.

Multiple Russian soldiers stepped forward with guns drawn. They stared at the group of child soldiers, mixed in with the set of young adults.

The front three Russians exchanged a few words. Then one of them took another step forward and in bad German ordered the German soldiers to take off their shirts while gesturing.

"SS hier! (SS here!)" he ordered, gesturing the way to his right with the rifle and "...Nicht-SS hier! (Non-SS here!) " pointing to his left. Everyone in this group had an SS tattoo. They all pretty much came together from being tattooed back in the Nuernberger SS HQ. None of the soldiers here were direct *Wehrmacht* or non-SS, at least not based on their marking. The young group of soldiers hesitated; they didn't want to be considered SS just because of the tattoo. The SS was known for its extreme brutality throughout the war, but these kids had no part of it. They all at the same time unbuttoned their worn out shirts and quickly pulled off their sleeve and lifted up their arms to reveal their SS tattoos.

The Russian soldier looked astonished when he realized all of them bore the SS tattoo. He exchanged a few words with the soldiers behind him, then moved closer and started to tap each "trench-digger" on his shoulder, now hand-sorting them by age. It became clear quickly that anyone who looked 18 or over he tapped and

ordered them to the left, and anyone who looked under 18 he sent over to the right. He ordered everyone around with his rifle.
Hans was sent to the left with the older group.
Karl was sent to the right.
"No!" Karl was trying to tell the Russian soldier, who in quick response pointed his rifle at Karl's face. Karl wanted to follow his brother to the left, but with the rifle pointed at him, he immediately quieted down, and with his hands up slowly walked over to the right.
Hans had always looked much older. He was tall for his age and broad shouldered, and it would be difficult for him to pass for younger than 18. He also had grown a blond mustache since he had arrived here, while Karl kept the few hairs that were growing on his face clean-shaven. The mustache made Hans look even older.
"Why couldn't he have shaved that thing off!" Karl was desperate, though not certain it would have made a difference.
He could not believe what had just happened. Karl and Hans kept looking over at each other, from their two separate lines, one more worried about the other, still with their hands up.
After less than 30 minutes, when all were sorted out, there were 230 young soldiers lined up on the right and the 40 older SS soldiers on the left, the rest had either fled or shot themselves.
"Marsch!" the Russian ordered the older group on the left to march back east, towards where they had come from. Two tanks, along with their assigned soldiers, turned around and led the way for this eastern convoy.

Karl still couldn't believe that Hans had been ordered to march with the older group. He witnessed his brother marching away a few rows behind Albert and the Oberfeldwebel Bertrandt. Karl felt the most helpless feeling he had ever felt. There was nothing he could do at this point. His brother didn't belong with them, but he now had to watch them take him away together with Albert, the SS fanatic. Hans was the polar opposite of Albert: he had believed in this war as little as Karl had.

The Russian soldiers ordered the youngsters on the right to march inland toward Linz, the remaining tank heading west with them, leading the young prisoners of war. What would they be doing in Linz? What would his brother be doing?

The agony for Karl to see his big brother march away with the rest of the older SS soldiers and those noisy tanks heading toward the east — the opposite direction he was going — almost brought him to his knees. He felt weak and nauseous. Karl held back tears of fear, frustration and helplessness.

Karl was only glad that his Mom was not witnessing this right now; she might have not survived this. Karl forced himself to remain strong because it wouldn't do Hans any good if he passed out right there. He tried to get back in control, breathing deep and letting the cold mountain air fill his lungs.

Karl kept turning his head around as he marched inland with the rest of the young soldiers. But the Russian guard soldier directly next to Karl scuffed him in the shoulder with the butt of his rifle, motioning for him to march forward.

In the split second that Karl turned around, trying to look back for his brother, he was certain that he saw Hans turn around, too. They were already too far in the distance to really make out a face exactly. *"Where are they taking him? Why would they march them east and us in the opposite direction? Why separate them from the rest?"* Deep in thought, he was startled when he heard the echo of a salvo of shots fired in the distance. Karl and the other soldiers instantly yanked around to frantically look in the direction of the fire. They could see a bunch of men lying on the ground in the distance there, executed by the Russian soldiers; though not all SS were shot, which was clear by the ones still standing in their grey SS uniform. Karl held his breath.

"Oh mein Gott, oh mein Gott (oh my God)!" that's all Karl could say. Shock and intense panic overcame him. They killed Hans! He attempted to run back east when a Russian soldier pointed the rifle directly at his torso.

"стоп!" he ordered Karl, dark-brown cold eyes staring at him. Karl froze instantly. He jerked his hands up and stared back. The rest of his group kept marching on, marching around Karl. Didn't anyone else care about these dead soldiers? Was Karl the only one with a relative in the other group? Had they all become numb inside over these past months?

"Mein Bruder (my brother)!" Karl tried to explain to the soldier, pointing with his face in the direction of the shots, still holding his hands up, while trying to hold back more tears. Complete panic had overcome him, and it took all of his self-control to not run toward

the other group. It was clear the Russian either didn't understand Karl or didn't care. He didn't budge, his rifle still pointed at Karl.
"брат! (Brother in Russian)" Alois, who had been further back, came up next to Karl and stopped to try and communicate with the Russian soldier. "брат," Alois repeated the word, to get the soldier to understand, not knowing whether he would.
The Russian soldier looked again at Karl, as if finally recognizing what he was saying. He also turned around for a split second to look in the direction of the distant older SS group. With the 20 or so soldiers lying dead, the rest of that group had continued to march on toward the east, armed Russian soldiers on each side.
Why weren't all the SS killed? Did they pick the oldest? Had one of them tried to flee? What would happen to the rest?
Karl pleaded, *"Mein Bruder, mein Bruder,"* still pointing with his face in the direction of the dead bodies, with his hands barely up, bent at the elbow.
The Russian soldier then turned back and directed Karl to turn around by making a motion with his rifle and to catch up to the rest of the group, which was marching down the hill in the direction of Linz. Karl and Alois had no other choice but to do just that with the rifle pointed at them. They ran to catch up with the group.
Karl swallowed hard to hold in the tears. Karl and Alois were now at the tail end of the large group of soldiers being marched downhill toward Linz. For each five rows of German soldiers five deep, there was a Russian soldier with a machine gun on each side. The young

German SS soldiers didn't stand any chance unarmed and to avoid being shot they had to march along.
"It will be OK, they probably didn't get Hans!" Alois whispered to Karl, trying to console him, while marching, both looking straight ahead. Karl's agonized tears streamed down his red cheeks, each tear creating another path on his unwashed dirty face.
"I think I saw him walk away with the leftover group." Alois' well-meaning attempts to appease him didn't register with Karl, instead his mind was racing as he kept marching in-step with Alois on auto-mode. From his Hitler-Jugend days, Karl learned to march, while his mind was somewhere else. They continued to close the formation of young SS soldiers marching down the hill.
"*How can I get back there and see who they shot? Will I ever see Hans again? Even if they killed him, I want to see him. I need to be sure. They can't just leave him lying there. What if he is just injured and needs help and is in terrible pain? Maybe they didn't kill him at all, because he is one of the youngest*?"
"Karl!" Alois hissed at Karl, realizing that Karl was not paying attention at all.
Back to the present for a moment, Karl looked straight ahead but whispered the impatient response, "What?" while continuing the marching cadence. After a while he murmured to Alois so the guards near them couldn't hear them, even though they didn't seem to speak any German:
"The Russians will kill us, too. I am not sure where they are taking us, but they will kill us the same way they killed them back there.

We need to get away as soon as we can!" Karl forged a plan, whispering.

"What do you mean? How?" whispered Alois, terrified and nervously excited at the same time, while continuing to march looking forward. Karl didn't respond, just stared straight ahead, and they all kept marching along the field toward Linz. Their path lead mostly downhill. A few kilometers down the country road they finally passed the faded yellow sign with black letters, "Welcome to Plesching."

They saw smoke in the distance, a smoldering farm.

"Russians!" Karl was sure, and wondered for a split second what exactly happened here. But his worry about his brother again took over.

Plesching was a quaint village on the outskirts of Linz, surrounded by the Alps. The houses sprinkled throughout the area were decorated with different shades of brown timber. Smoke slithered out of a few chimneys, but the village looked deserted. The church bells rang violently, warning the villagers that a large group of Russian soldiers was approaching, though they probably could not have missed the noise of the loud squeaking tanks leading the soldiers heading towards them.

The group marched along the village's main road, which wound uphill. It was getting hard to keep up. The captured soldiers were cold, hungry and weak. *Where are they taking us?* Karl thought through the cadence. *Maybe to some sort of Russian make-shift internment camp?*

"Where do you think they are they taking us?" Karl heard himself asking out loud to Alois, who was still next to him. It was a rhetorical question. Karl realized no one around him knew the answer, and the Russians wouldn't tell him. No response. Alois just shrugged his shoulder, he would only be guessing, and everyone was just marching along, entrenched in their own scared and worried thoughts, one more exhausted and hungry than the other.

The paved village road was covered in patches of dried up cow dung, leftovers from herding the cows to the pastures. It now wound left, where it narrowed with the old houses framing each side of the road. The captives along with their capturers marched along. For just a moment the guards on each side were a few rows ahead of them.

"Run!" Karl hissed to Alois, and without much thought Karl darted behind the house to his left. Alois' reflexively copied Karl's moves and took chase. Not ever turning around, they keep running, zig-zag, as if being chased by an army, expecting to be shot at any second, sprinting past house after house, running through shrubberies, a couple times jumping over fences, running for their lives.

Completely out of breath, they arrived at the end of the tiny village. They heard a dog's angry bark in the distance. The houses had given them protection from sight, but then they had to run across an open field lined by woods. While still running, Karl for the first time turned around to see if anyone was chasing them. But there was no one, and so he and Alois sprinted across the open field as if running the biggest race of their life toward the thick underwood and trees at the end of the field that would give them much-needed coverage.

When they were finally shielded behind trees, Karl stopped for just a quick moment. Heaving and looking back again, he was surprised. "Did they not notice?" he barely got the question out and he was breathing so hard, his lungs felt like they were burning.
"I am not sure!" Alois was near panic, and also out of breath.
Karl expected to be chased and to be shot at, but he knew they needed to get away. Laying down in the moss covered ground, they looked back to where they had come from, scanning the open field through the trees – their chests still moving up and down. "I don't trust it. It's too quiet. Where should we go?" Alois asked in panic.
"Shhhh. Let's just wait here for a bit. Wait and see if they come for us." Karl whispered, winded and exhausted, his chest moving up and down.
They both cowered there quietly for a few more minutes, frantically watching and listening for any movement.
Karl whispered on, without losing sight. "Let's see if we can find a farmer who can hide us, because you know the Russians will start looking for us. They will notice we are missing, if they haven't already. … But first we need to go back to the field and see if they killed ..." Karl stopped right there and then finished with, "Let's see who they killed."
Alois didn't respond, still plopped down next to Karl. They sat up for a few minutes and continued to scour the direction they came from. There was no movement at all, just empty fields with a few cows whose mooing could be heard. There was a light wind. The

dog was still barking in the distance. Nobody seemed to be after them.

"I don't trust the silence," Karl said and jumped up again. "Let's go!" Before Alois could respond, Karl took the uphill path that would lead them back to the spot where they had been captured.

"Pass auf! (Be careful!)" Alois hissed. "What if they expect us there? Can't we just hide here for a few hours?"

"No, and why would they?" Karl was now sprinting again. He needed to find out whether his brother lay dying in that field or worse, whether he was dead. Nothing could stop him. Alois followed suit.

When they finally got back to the open field where they had been taken into captivity just little over an hour ago, the wind was howling more eerily than before. The land was elevated, and it was definitely colder than in the village. There was nothing there but dried up field and few flowers dotted throughout the grass. They saw the bodies lying in the distance where they witnessed them being shot earlier. Karl sped up. The wind was blowing hard, as if to hold them back. Alois was right behind him.

As they got closer, Karl slowed down to hold up his sleeve across his mouth and almost covered his eyes. He was afraid of what he was going to see. Alois walked hesitatingly next to him. Before they got there, Alois reminded Karl, "I don't think Hans is here, I am sure I saw him marching away with the rest, I recognize his broad-shouldered walk!" Karl wanted to agree with Alois. His gut feeling said that Alois might be right, he also thought for a split second that he saw Hans walk away with the rest, but he needed to be one hundred percent sure.

Finally standing in front of the fallen bodies, they immediately recognized Feldwebel Bertrand's body lying there with eyes open, blood dried to the side of his mouth and neck. Anton's dead body was lying right next to Bertrand and the rest of the soldiers. No one moved, not a single sound besides the brisk wind and a few crows in the distance could be heard.

One soldier lay face down. Karl slowly walked toward him and got down on his knees to turn him over: It was Albert. He looked peaceful, the stern look he had maintained since becoming an SS was wiped away. Albert had said the Russians would move forward only over his dead body. What a self-fulfilling prophecy! Though Karl didn't wish for Albert to die this way, if anything he would have wanted for Albert to have to pay in the court of law but not be killed by Russians. Deep sympathy for his former playmate overcame him. The Nazi's had brainwashed him. Karl remembered the few good times he had with Albert and before he grew into this insane SS fanatic. He didn't want to spend too much more time thinking about how sad it was for his former neighbor to have turned out like that. What would have happened to Albert if it wasn't for this war? Would Albert have gone on to learn a trade like his father, who had been a fine butcher until he had also became an SS fanatic? Wasted lives. A wasted war.

Karl took a step back over and leaned down to close Feldwebel Bertrandt's eyes. The Feldwebel had been a respectable person.

Though he only did what he was told, he had treated everyone with as much dignity as he had in him.

"Let's feel everyone's pulse!" Alois suggested, though they knew all were dead. He and Karl quickly grabbed the wrists of one soldier after another to check for life.

No pulse on any of them could be felt.

The sight of all the dead and bloodied bodies in front of them was vastly disturbing and frightening, and it would be imprinted in Karl's memory forever. He also felt relief and then instant guilt at that sense of relief, but … his brother Hans was not one of the dead! Karl started feeling hopeful. Maybe Hans could also escape? Karl looked east, wondering how close Hans and his group was.

As if reading his mind, Alois responded, "No, we can't go after them."

"I know," Karl responded, resigned. "We are outnumbered. I know!"

"We need to bury them!" decided Karl.

"No, we need to get out of here! Look, everyone can see us kilometers away, we just need to hide!" Alois was frantic.

Karl looked around, still nobody in sight only empty space, with the beautiful Alps lining the background. But the scenic view didn't register in Karl's mind.

"Let's just move them into the trench over there and put dirt over them. They deserve to be buried. We can't leave them here like this." Karl decided.

"The people from the village will eventually find and bury them!" Alois pleaded and attempted to yank Karl away so they could get going.

"We don't even know when that will be." Karl ignored Alois' protest, rolled up his sleeves, bent down and grabbed Feldwebel Bertrandt's corpse by his boots and started dragging it toward the freshly dug trench nearby.

Karl thought of the irony. *"None of the dead soldiers imagined this morning when they were digging this trench that they were actually digging their grave.*"

Karl sighed heavily. Exhausted, he used all the strength his young, malnourished body could provide to do the arduous work. Once finished with Feldwebel Bertrandt's body, he trekked back for the next dead soldier. Reluctantly, Alois grabbed Anton's body by the boots and did the same. They arranged all the dead soldiers next to each other in the trench and once the last soldier was lined up, they start shoveling dirt over them.

"Mmmmmmmmmmmm."

"What was that?"

"Moaning?"

Alois dropped his spade, and stunned they both stopped immediately.

They heard it again. "Mmmmmmmmmm."

"Over there, it's coming from over there," Karl pointed in the direction of the noise.

"It's Anton, the moan is coming from Anton!" Alois screamed frantically.

They ran back over to Anton and bent down over him to inspect him close-up: Anton's left pant pocket was blood soaked. Karl ripped off his own jacket, shirt and undershirt and used the undershirt to press it against the wound. He didn't feel the cold air. Anton moaned louder in a delirium, clearly in immense pain.

"Mein Gott!" said Karl. "He is still alive! We need to get him help. Let's take him to one of the Bauernhoefe (farms) we passed on the way here! Let's see if they can help."

Alois rolled his eyes. How could they do this without the Russians catching up with them? They needed to get themselves into safety first.

"We have to try!" Karl insisted.

Before they left, Karl quickly took the largest branch he could find and dug it into the half-finished grave to serve as a marker. It was more important to take Anton back to see if someone in the village could help than to finish this grave.

They both stood silently over the dead for a few seconds, quietly folding their hands for a quick prayer, then in a hurry they quickly crossed themselves and switched their focus back to Anton.

"Someone can give them a more deserving burial later on," Karl said, determined to make sure the villagers would find them. "We'll tell the next person in the village we see about this."

Karl scooped up Anton under both arms. He was so heavy that Karl's knees nearly buckled from the weight.

"Anton – It's Karl and Alois – we are here to get you some help!" Karl tried to comfort Anton, though he couldn't be sure that Anton heard him.
Anton kept moaning, barely conscious.
"We will take turns. I'll carry him for a while then you," Karl forged the plan.
Alois still tried to protest. "We could leave Anton here to get help. Then send someone come back here to get him!"
"How do you know we'll find anyone willing to help? If this was your brother or my brother Hans, would you still say that? We have an obligation to take him and try to save him now!" Karl's mind was made up.
By then the sun had moved west. It was way past lunch time and their stomachs were really feeling the emptiness. "Mensch, he is heavy! I am starving and parched!" Karl complained as he continued walking with the heavy load of Anton, who was getting heavier with each step.
"When we ran here, did you see that farmhouse off to the left all by itself with the smoking chimney?"
"Yes, I also saw the one that was still smoldering. Did you see that one?" Alois hinted at the Russians being nearby.
Yes, Karl recalled seeing that burned down farmhouse, too, but now his focus was on the other farmhouse that was surrounded by more land than the rest of them, plus the smoking chimney indicating someone had to be home.

"How far are the Russians from that farm?" "Why was one farm burned down but not the other?" The worried thoughts kept flying. While carrying Anton, Karl strategized. "Let's go back there and see if the farmer can help with Anton, maybe give us some food, get us out of this uniform, and hide us for a couple of days."

"OK," mumbled Alois in agreement. They didn't know whether anyone would even be home and would let them come inside or instead perhaps shoot at them? They both realized trying to get help there was their only option. Anton needed immediate help and they needed to get out of these uniforms.

Karl and Alois switched off schlepping Anton. The hike back to the farmhouse was exhausting, and a couple of times they nearly gave up, wanting to just put Anton down leaving him lying there on the spot. But step by step they kept at it, firing each other on, when either one was ready to quit. Sometimes, they carried him together, other times alone. Ten minutes at a time was the maximum each could handle. They counted the seconds out loud for each other… 1, 2, 3, …. That kept their mind off the strenuous task, then they switched again. Anton's moaning slowed, and they worried he wouldn't make it. It took them almost twice as long to get back to where they earlier passed the farmhouse. When they finally arrived there, Karl ran ahead and took the cement steps leading to the front white door in twos and banged at it with both fists.

No answer! Karl could see the white smoke still slithering out of the chimney and the cows grazing in the grass behind the house. He was certain someone had to be home.

Karl knocked again, this time even louder. They waited another few minutes. Finally the door squeaked open just a crack. A middle-aged woman in a flowered apron peeked through the opened small space. Her kind brown eyes studied Karl, but then she saw Alois with bloodied Anton in his arms downstairs right behind and she quickly swung the door wide open.

"Oh mein Gott, what is going on?" She threw her hand in front of her lips at the sight and immediately rushed down the steps to help Alois carry Anton. "What happened? Hurry! Come inside! *Schnell, schnell"*

Karl stepped back down, too, to help Alois get Anton up the steps, and the woman quickly hushed the boys inside and rushed to close the door shut. They stepped into the warm, cozy home. The smell of freshly baked bread lingered in the air. The living room they were standing in was connected to a dining room. An old, worn out green upholstered couch and a brown table covered by a flowered tablecloth, surrounded by a wooden bench decorated the room; on the other end of this large room was the kitchen. Nestled at the corner of the kitchen was a rustic black-iron wood burning stove with a teakettle sitting on top of it, whistling the steam out of it. Lining the white kitchen wall was a scratched up cupboard.

The woman sped over to move the whistling teakettle to the side. Then she turned around and said : "I will get a blanket for him and some cloths." She rushed out and quickly returned with a blanket. She hurriedly spread it on the couch and set the cloths on it, immediately directing them while pointing to the couch:

"Put him on here, carefully!" Alois and Karl worked together to let Anton down gently.

Let's see what we can do here," sitting down on the couch next to Anton and leaning in to him, she unbuttoned his uniform jacket, and then looked at his left side covered in crusted blood. The undershirt Karl had used to stop the bleeding was blood soaked. With the help of the boys, she removed the pants and inspected the wound. The bleeding seemed to have stopped. "I'll take boiled water with some salt in it and at least try to clean out the wound. I am not a nurse, but I know the wound should be cleaned," she mumbled nervously as she headed for the kitchen side of the room with the cloths in her hand. She poured water from the teakettle into a bowl, grabbed some salt from the old cupboard and mixed it with the water and dunked the cloths into it. For a second Karl was impressed that these farmers still had salt. He hadn't tasted any in months. She then walked over to Anton and dabbed the soaked cloth around the wound. Anton seemed deeply asleep – he was not making any sounds. She felt for his pulse and could barely feel it. But at least he was still alive.

The two boys were standing there watching her helplessly.

The woman again jumped up and ran toward the back of the kitchen to open a door that led downstairs. "Wilhelm!!" she screamed.

"Schnell, Wilhelm, come upstairs"

"What?" a deep grumpy sounding voice responded as they heard fast footsteps coming up from the barn. Within seconds a burley, sandy haired, tall middle-aged man dressed in blue overalls and a faded white under-shirt walked through the door.

“What is this?” Astounded, he looked at Karl and Alois standing there by the couch with half-undressed and blood-stained Anton lying on it. A shadow fell over his face *“Mein Gott*, who are they?” he looked at his wife accusingly, irritated and at the same time scared.

“Look at them, they are kids, they need help!” she responded, trying to calm him.

Wilhelm turned to Karl and Alois and demanded, “What is going on? What happened to him?” motioning with his large beard-stubbled chin at Anton, lying on the coach. “Who are you?”

“Did you hear the war is over? Hitler killed himself,” Alois jumped in.

“Yes, I heard on the radio!” Wilhelm responded, letting Alois sidetrack him for a split second.

“But what happened to you all? Why are you here in my house? Have Russians followed you?” he asked.

Anxiously Wilhelm stepped over to one of the kitchen windows, slightly pushing aside the curtains, peering outside to see whether anyone had followed them. Then he moved over to the living room window and did the same.

“Nobody has followed us!” Karl responded firmly, though he couldn’t be sure himself. He felt a twinge of guilt about possibly endangering this couple. What if the Russians were still looking for them? He started talking as fast as he could, everything he had kept bottled up in his mind the last couple of months was pouring out. He explained all the details, introducing himself and Alois, and how they were grabbed from their homes by the SS, how they were indoctrinated into the SS without any specific training, how they were digging trenches the last months up the hill not far from here, how he even spent a few days at the front, how just a few hours ago they were captured by the Russians, and how Anton was shot by the Russians along with the others, left for dead, about his brother, how they fled the Russians, and ... then …

Wilhelm stopped him. "You can't stay here!"

The boys look at him, scared.

"Wilhelm!" The wife tried to object.

But the farmer went on: "A neighbor farmer was shot and killed yesterday. Did you see that burned farmhouse just down the hill? It is still smoldering. That was his farmhouse. I heard Wassermann, the farmer, was shot on the spot. He had been hiding three German SS soldiers and the Russians found them. They killed Wassermann and his family and burned his farm down. It is much too dangerous for my wife and me to hide you here! The Russians have been raping and murdering. They are animals. I don't think there is a female in town who hasn't been raped by them." He looked at Lisl, who was looking down.

"Except Lisl so far! She is one of the few! We want to keep it that way! And we want to stay alive!"

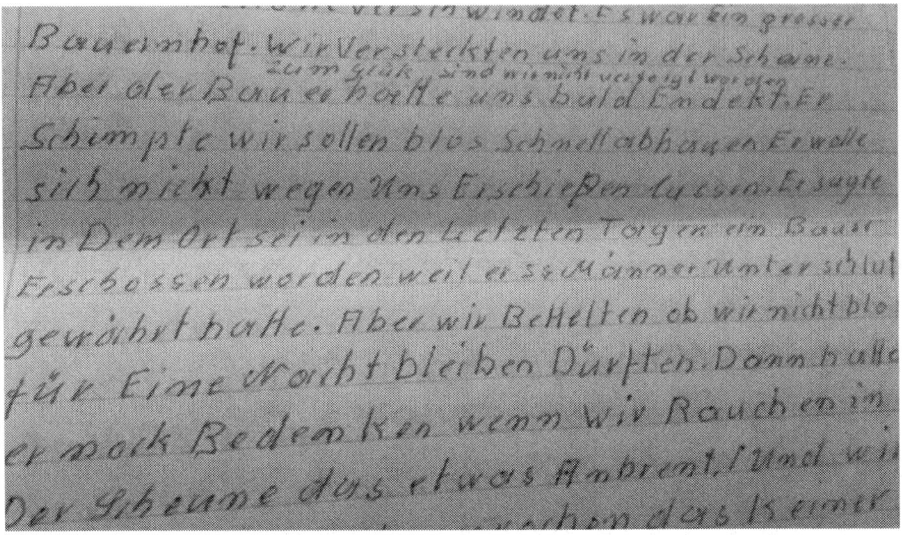
... verschwindet. Es war ein grosser
Bauernhof. Wir versteckten uns in der Scheune.
Zum Glück sind wir nicht verfolgt worden
Aber der Bauer hatte uns bald Endeckt. Er
Schimpfte wir sollen blos Schnell abhauen Er wolle
sich nicht wegen Uns Erschießen lassen. Er sagte
in Dem Ort sei in den letzten Tagen ein Bauer
Erschossen worden weil er 5 Männer Unterschlupf
gewährt hatte. Aber wir Bettelten ob wir nicht blo
für Eine Nacht bleiben Dürften. Dann hatte
er noch Bedenken wenn wir Rauchen in
Der Scheune das etwas Anbrent. Und wi

His wife jumped in, pleading "Look at the boy," pointing toward Anton, now on the couch. "He is severely injured, he needs help. Give them one night. I'll give them something to eat; they are starving. They can borrow some of Markus' clothes, and we send them off first thing in the morning. Just give them one night. One night's good rest and a good meal! Wouldn't you want someone to help Markus if he needed help now?"

Karl and Alois held their breath, eagerly anticipating Wilhelm's response. Karl wondered fleetingly who Markus was, but came to the conclusion he must be their son. Wilhelm stared at his wife as if his immediate reaction was to say no, but then looked at Anton again, as if he just realizing the bad shape he was in. He let out air. Sighing and defeated, he agreed, "Alright, but one night only! You absolutely have to leave before daylight! Nobody can see you leave this farm! I hope no one saw you coming here."

Karl and Alois exhaled, relieved for the moment. They could figure something else out tomorrow. That would give them one more night away from the Russians. Maybe their captors had given up searching for them or better yet haven't even noticed they were missing. But Karl knew that the Russian soldier who pointed the gun at him when he wanted to chase after Hans, would remember him. Their eyes had locked.

"I am Elisabeth Bauer," the woman said, trying a slight smile, "just call me Lisl." She walked up to each and shook the boys' hands. "And this is my husband, Wilhelm" She smiled as she grabbed her husband's arm.

"Maybe we can get Doctor Weinsteiger to come, Wilhelm?" She looked at her husband pleadingly, and before he could respond she explained to the boys, "Weinsteiger is retired, but he can help here more than any of us. He lives just a few farmhouses over. We can trust him."

Wilhelm reluctantly agreed and said he'd take his bike over to see if he could get Dr. Weinsteiger to come over immediately.

Wilhelm again reminded the boys not to leave the house until it was either pitch dark or first thing in the morning, before sun-up. He reiterated that it would be deadly for them all if they were caught harboring soldiers.

The boys assured him they were not planning to go anywhere in daylight.

Wilhelm slammed the door shut, and they could hear him lock it behind him and then his heavy footsteps racing down the steps.

Lisl offered the boys slices of that big brown loaf of bread sitting on the kitchen counter on a Edelweiss-flowered plate.

"Can I have some water first?" Karl was so relieved she would offer them something to eat.

"Oh, of course! You are thirsty."

"Get some glasses," she pointed in the direction of the old wooden/glass kitchen cupboard. "Get water from the bucket over there, it's fresh from the well."

The two obliged and quickly gulped two glasses of water in a row. "I would like to get a slice of that bread, please," Alois asked politely.

"Of course, take it!" she offered.

Fresh out of the oven, the bread was still warm and soft and its scent continued to fill the air. They hadn't eaten fresh bread since they were snatched from their homes. Alois was from a nearby town called Bamberg, only 50 km away from Karl's hometown.

The young men devoured the bread to its last crumb. "Some fresh milk is there too. I boiled it; the skin is still on top. Let me strain it." With that, Lisl strained the milk into two mugs. "Here, it's still warm."

Fresh baked bread and warm milk, Karl was sure he had never eaten any food this good.

"And when you are finished with that, I have some *Most* (alcoholic apple cider) if you want." Lisl continued to spoil them.

"*Most*?" Karl and Alois' eyes widened. Yes, they would love some.

Lisl poured them each a glass. This was a feast, and more food and drink in one sitting than they both had consumed in over seven months.

In the background, they heard Anton's slight groans. He seemed to come to again. Maybe he didn't want to be left alone. Lisl walked over and touched Anton's arm lightly. "You will be alright," she said softly. Karl and Alois savored the warm milk. There was not much they could do for Anton except wait. Lisl was providing all the comfort they could garner at that point. Hopefully Wilhelm would come back with that doctor soon.

Lisl left the kitchen through another door opposite the kitchen leading upstairs and a few moments later came back, her arms loaded with men's pants and shirts, socks and two pairs of shoes. She could barely balance it all in her arms.

"Here, see if these fit you." She set the clothes and shoes down on the wooden bench next to the dining room table when one of the shoes dropped onto the wooden floor. Alois quickly jumped to pick it up for her. "Thanks! We need to get you out of these uniforms." The boys looked at her inquisitively, and as if she could read their minds she explained: "These clothes belong to Markus, our son. He was sent to the Eastern Front in 1943, and we haven't heard from him in over a year. He used to write us letters, but we haven't received any from him since early 1944." For a minute she looked up at the picture of her son in his Wehrmacht uniform hanging on the wall, as if by studying his picture, she could get answers about his fate.

"See if his clothes can help you at least." She changed the subject.

“How old is Markus?” Alois asked concerned.

“He turned 24 two months ago.” Lisl looked down, but Karl could see the sadness that had overcome her face. “Another one of his birthdays we have missed.”

Karl and Alois looked at each other, knowing that if one hasn’t heard from their kin in such a long time, the chances of him coming back were low.

“Change already!” she ordered them, forcing herself to snap out of the moment of sadness that had overcome her.

Quickly they stepped away into the back of the living room, turning away, and then tore off their uniforms, so happy to get rid of them. Then they rushed to put on the new clothes.

It was such a relief to again be in civilian clothes.

Karl looked around to see if anyone was watching, but Lisl was looking the opposite direction to give them privacy. He sneaked the pocket knife out of his uniform pant pocket into his new civilian pants pocket. How did the Russians not check whether he had any weapons, regardless how small? Karl had been lucky.

The clothes fit a bit loose and baggy on Alois, but fit Karl near perfectly and while the shoes were a bit big on Alois, they were almost too tight for Karl, but the fit was close enough. They were just happy to be in civilian clothes again. Alois rolled up the pant legs and sleeves each twice.

Lisl picked up their dirty uniform pants and jackets from the floor and walked the pile over to the wood stove to shove in the first pair of pants. “We have to burn all evidence,” she winked in their direction, "one piece at a time. We should get the rest of the clothes off Anton, too, once the doctor is here, we can work on that."

Not even 20 minutes had passed when Wilhelm unlocked the door and rushed inside, shutting it swiftly behind him. Was he being followed? He carefully peeked behind each curtain again to make sure he wasn't. Then he excitedly, but in a hushed tone, proclaimed that Dr. Weinsteiger was on his way.

"I found him sweeping his barn. He will be right over." And looking at the boys, he ordered, "You boys need to go hide in the barn right now!" Wilhelm sternly pointed to the direction of the barn downstairs and adjacent to their house.

"Grab a few blankets for them, Lisl, but they need to hide in the barn, and they need to stay there throughout the night. Before sunlight, you both need to be out of here. We know Dr. Weinsteiger well, but nowadays you can't trust anyone completely. It's bad enough we will have to make up something about how we found this guy," Wilhelm nodded toward Anton, "but Dr. Weinsteiger doesn't need to be burdened knowing about you two."

Lisl came back with grey, rough looking woolen blankets and handed one to each boy.

"Don't sleep near the barn entrance, hide behind the haystacks as far back as possible," she advised them. She sounded worried. "And when you leave in the morning, make sure you stay away from Russian territory. You have to run west for at least 15 kilometers through the forest and always keep to the right. Then you'll come to a road; walk up it a few kilometers and you will see the railroad tracks. You will have to cross them, and then keep walking and you'll be in American (sovereign) territory (Amerikanisches Hoheitsgebiet).

"One more thing," Wilhelm now somberly jumped in. "Together with our priest we'll find that spot you've described where the dead soldiers are, and we'll make sure to give them a worthy burial."

That was one of the most comforting things Wilhelm could have told them. That farmer and his wife were good people. Karl and Alois were now eager to hide in the barn. They didn't want to get the farmer couple into any trouble, especially not after they had been treated so well by them.

"Now listen, and do what Lisl said!" Wilhelm ordered. "Go as far back and up in the barn as you can!"

Lisl ran back to the kitchen and quickly returned with two warm potatoes for each boy.

"Here a little bit more food for you two!" she smiled as she handed them the potatoes.

Karl put half of one in his mouth, bit down and with that and the blankets and the rest of the potatoes in their hands, the boys headed through the back kitchen door downstairs through another door that led them into the barn attached to the farm.

"Do you think the Russians are still looking for these boys?" Lisl whispered to Wilhelm nervously.

"I have a feeling they are."

In the barn, Karl and Alois walked across squeaky wooden planks covering the barn floor, passing spades, pitchforks and ladders hanging on the side of the timber wall. They climbed over haystack after piled haystack as far back and as high as they could; as far away from the front barn entrance door as possible. When they finally were in the farthest and highest corner of the barn, Karl moved one of the hay stacks in front of them. Their hideout was complete. They tried to make themselves comfortable, though the hay was starting to make them itch. Karl spread out his blanket to lie on, and they used Alois' blanket to cover themselves. They quickly ate the rest of the potatoes, and completely exhausted, they both started to drift off.

"I wonder how Hans is doing." Karl asked before completely nodding off.

"I am sure he is fine," appeased Alois. "Let's go to sleep!"

Within a few minutes they fell into a deep slumber. The unbelievable happenings of the day had left them exhausted.

"Где они, Где они." ("Where are they?)"

Karl's eyes flashed open, ripped awake by Russian sounds. Karl and Alois, immediately wide awake, looked at each other in sheer fear. Early sunlight was already streaming inside the barn.

They must have overslept, and the Russians were here looking for them!

Karl puts his finger across his lips to motion to Alois to be quiet. He pulled out the knife from his pocket. They both didn't dare to move; they tried to hold their breath. It sounded like there were at least two

Russian soldiers, if not three. The voices were coming closer; they were climbing toward them on the haystacks. The boys could hear pitchforks stabbing inside the haystack.

They were here to get them!

Crouching down as low as possible, Karl and Alois quietly scooted back until they felt the back barn wall. Now there was no more room for them to move. Karl had his knife in his hand, ready, though it was only a small pocket knife.

They heard them coming closer and closer, stabbing the haystacks over and over until they could actually see a pitchfork stabbing through the hay stack in front of them. Karl's heart skipped a beat. They both held their breaths.

They heard one of the Russians say something to the other, standing right next to them, only three haystacks separating them. A few moments of silence followed, the boys were still barely breathing.

A loud crash could be heard outside. Something large had collapsed or dropped.

What was it? Silence followed. After a few seconds, Karl could hear the Russians talk again, but now the voices seemed a bit further away. It sounded as if they had turned back. The pitchforks stabbing the haystacks had also stopped. The voices slowly started moving away farther and farther.

Karl and Alois looked at each other. Then they sat there quietly, without a word for what seemed like an eternity. Was anyone still there?

They still didn't dare to move for a while, even though they had not heard any more sounds for the past ten minutes.

Finally they slowly peeked from behind the bales and then barely dared to move, climbing slowly up front over the haystacks, still cautiously checking whether anyone was left inside the barn. They could see that the front barn door was wide open, and nobody was inside any longer. The Russians seemed to have given up and left.

"We have to go!" Karl whispered, and without waiting for a response he continued climbing back over the pile of haystacks down toward the barn front door. They stopped to look out the small window located high up on the side of the barn. The haystacks were piled so high that they only had to step on their tiptoes to see outside the high-up window. The angle didn't allow them to see anyone directly under the window and not much to the sides of it, they could only see fields and clear sky for miles straight ahead.

"Let's go. I think they are gone!" Karl was still whispering, and they both kept climbing down to the front of the barn. When they got to the door, they carefully glanced around the barn door and quickly looked left and right to make sure the Russians were really gone.

"Look!" exclaimed Alois and pointed to the south down the hill. Specks of three soldiers could be made out walking far in the distance. Karl and Alois ducked back inside. They didn't want one of them to turn around and see them.

"They are walking toward the village! Let's go the opposite, back east and then we'll follow the directions west through the woods just how Frau Lisl described them!" After waiting a bit longer inside the barn door, Karl and Alois confirmed one last time that the Russian soldiers had completely disappeared from sight.

The boys then darted out of the barn and ran up the hill into the woods. Out of the corners of his eyes, Karl could see the farmhouse's curtains move. He was sure Lisl and Wilhelm had been watching all that happened from their windows. How relieved they must have been to see everyone go away.

Karl felt incredibly guilty that they stayed into the morning light. How did they not wake up earlier? How could they have put the nice farmer and his wife into such danger? It must have been the Most. They should have never even drank that one glass, though Lisl had meant well.

They were lucky the Russians didn't find them. It was so close, and if they had found them they would have certainly shot them and the farmer and his wife on the spot. The barn and farmhouse would be burning right now. Karl would forever be thankful to Wilhelm, the farmer, and his wife, Lisl, who took them in for one night, and who gave them food and civilian clothes. Lisl would be forever remembered as the kindest woman Karl had met throughout all of the war. They didn't know what would happen to Anton. Maybe the couple hid Anton somewhere, maybe the Russian soldiers only looked for them in the barn? Was the doctor able to help Anton?

The boys continued to run through the woods. The plan was to stay inside the deep forest as long as they could, but always head west. The goal was to get away from the Eastern Front where the Russians were advancing. They drank water from a creek and ate a few barely ripe berries. They tasted some of the raw nettle they found, but it tasted even more bitter than they were used to. Karl didn't want to risk another night of diarrhea like the one at the front. His stomach had hurt so badly that night that he wasn't sure he would make it. Karl spit out the raw nettle, telling Alois his unripe green apple story at the front and the pain and bathroom consequences. They both needed to stay healthy. Alois also spit the nettle back out. They kept moving along until they stumbled onto large clusters of blueberries: everywhere they could see there were bushes of them. "My favorite berry!" Karl said as he quickly bent down to pick them by the handful and shove them into his mouth. "Mmmmh!" Alois also showed his approval as he also started to chomp down on them. Those were some of the sweetest blueberries they remembered ever eating. Their lips turned blue from the tasty berries and after twenty minutes of eagerly feasting on them, Karl pushed to keep going. As much as he would have wanted to eat every berry in sight, they had to get away from the Russian zone. They kept walking, but often took breaks, sitting there on the moss wondering what their future would entail. Karl's shoes now were really pinching his toes and he started to feel the blisters that had developed on his heels. They were too far away from home. Walking out in the open, even in civilian clothes they could be stopped by the Russians.

They felt somewhat safe deep in the woods. Surely the Russians wouldn't come that far in, their tanks couldn't get through all those big pine trees, though they were on guard for foot soldiers who could eventually cross their paths. They spent most of the day in the woods. When they didn't sit to rest, they walked west for about 15 km and then stepped outside the forest's awning to walk down the road for a few kilometers, following the directions Lisl had given them. There was still no railroad crossing in sight. The sun was starting to set and they started to worry, when they finally stumbled on to the railroad tracks.

Excitedly, they crossed them. The directions Lisl had given them were simple to follow. A few kilometers after crossing the old tracks they walked inside the forest parallel to a dirt road.

They heard trucks in the distance!

They immediately darted back inside the forest, and crouched behind large pine trees to wait and see whether it was another Russian convoy.

"Americans!" Alois recognized the American flag.

"Americans! Americans!" Karl screamed. "Let's surrender!"

Karl pulled out his pocket knife and dug it into the moss at the spot where they were squatting and left it there for good.

"Let's go!" Karl jumped up with his hands up and ran up the dirt road, and Alois was right behind him. Karl hissed at him, "Your hands!" and Alois quickly obliged. They both walked toward the American convoy with their hands up high.

What a sight that must have been for the American GIs. These young boys, Karl only 16 and Alois only 17, dressed in civilian clothes, with blue lips, and holding their hands up high to surrender. The leading trucker in the convoy put on the brakes hard, and the soldier walking next to it kept his rifle ready and walked up to the boys. "Do you speak English?"

"Nein! Kein Englisch" was all Karl could respond with. He didn't speak any English, but understood enough of it to respond to this sentence.

The soldier hollered at another soldier further back in the convoy: "Sgt. Fritz, come up here! I need you to translate." Quickly another soldier stepped forward toward the group of soldiers who were surrounding the two young boys.

Sgt. Fritz, in perfect German, asked the boys: *"Seid ihr bewaffnet?* (Are you armed?)"

"No," they responded in unison.

"Roll up your sleeves!" Sgt. Fritz knew to look for the SS tattoo — enough kid and adult SS have surrendered to them. Both Karl and Alois rolled up their sleeves and revealed their SS tattoos.

Karl told them quickly their story and how they were fleeing the Russian soldiers, who were pilfering and killing and burning farmer's houses down.

Sgt. Fritz just nodded knowingly: "Yes, they are animals! OK, come with us!"

Sgt. Fritz translated for his staff-sergeant that the boys were dragged into the SS against their will.

"Look at them, they are kids!"

"That's what they all say. They are SS! We'll have to take them to the SS camp."

That day Karl and Alois became American prisoners of war. Though they were somewhat relieved, they didn't know what would await them next.

Chapter 8

Camp

After Karl and Alois had surrendered to the Americans, the GIs had brought the two boys to a POW camp, to a set of barracks previously used by the German *Abwehr* (defense) near Linz. The site was quickly turning into a makeshift camp for the younger German POWs who were arriving daily.

After they had been in American captivity for only a few days, there were already one hundred young soldiers, and Karl quit counting. The barracks were quickly surrounded by a sea of temporary American Army military tents and some Red Cross tents.

The German-speaking Sgt. Fritz had explained to Karl and Alois that they would have to follow orders and work for the American GIs. They each were asked their personal information, such as their first and last name, any crafts or skills, and more. Karl, for the first time in a long time, mentioned his nearly finished carpentry apprenticeship. The Americans didn't ask about their addresses or their parents; for now they were only POWs. Then, without explanation, Alois and Karl were separated — Karl was given quarters in one end of the barracks and Alois on the other end of the camp. The Americans must have figured that each of them on their own would be less prone to scheming, though both boys were way too hungry and too far from home to do anything but what they were told. After all, they had surrendered in fear of the Russians.

Karl was moved into a barracks room with a young SS named Max, who had surrendered to the American GIs a few days earlier. A few days later, Wilfried and Frederick were added. The bunk beds filled quickly, and some of the captured had to sleep on the floor. Fights over beds would become common. Karl pleaded with the GIs to not add any additional POWs to their already crowded room. At this rate they would kill each other over a bed.

Each of the captives had similar stories to tell: They were all teenagers, pulled into the war around six months ago. They were all tired and hungry because they also had been running from the Russians. There was a common sense of relief that they had been "captured" by the Americans instead of the Russians. All of them had heard about the Russian atrocities. Once-captured SS soldiers were shot on the spot, or worse, slowly tortured to their deaths. Some had witnessed this cruelty with their own eyes, but all had heard about the massacres. Not until much later would the young soldiers learn that the German soldiers on the Russian front were equally atrocious, and much of this inhumane treatment was considered payback by the Russians.

The captured teenagers were all desperate to go home. Hitler was dead. The war in Germany was over — a war none of these young kids chose to fight — and they were eager to find out the whereabouts of their loved ones. Wilfried kept talking about how much he missed his mom. Frederick really missed his younger brother. Everyone else wondered what happened to his family. Karl just listened to all of them telling similar stories after he had grown tired of telling his own.

How long would they be held in this makeshift American prison camp? How long would the Americans stay here? Would they take over the German government? The Americans sure were far away from home but Karl would be fine with the Americans being in charge of Germany, though he didn't know what that would entail. America, in his mind, had always been this glamorous, faraway country to which many Germans had emigrated.

Although he was only 8 years old in 1936, Karl recalled the excitement by Opa and Mutter during the Olympics as they cheered on the black Olympian, Jesse Owens, who won the long jump gold medal against the German rival Carl Ludwig "Luz" Long. Hitler had wanted to show the world how the Aryan race would beat everyone in the Olympic Games, but Jesse Owens proved otherwise. Much to the displeasure of Hitler, the German star Luz Long became friends with Jesse Owens. When the American won one of his four Olympic gold medals, Luz even ran a victory lap with him. According to Long's mother Rudolph Hess, appointed Deputy Führer to Adolf Hitler, then instructed Luz to never hug a "Neger" (Negro) again. Unfortunately, Luz was later sent to the front (many thought it was to punish him), where he was killed. The German public adored Jesse Owens, and he was the epitome of an American to Karl: Karl expected most Americans to be athletic and impressive like Jesse.

In the American prison camp, twice a day the boys were fed stale bread and watery soup with some potatoes but mostly unidentifiable chunks floating in it. This was not nearly enough nourishment for growing boys, but their youth was what continued to help them get through these starving days. While the sun spread warmth during the day, at night the barrack walls were not thick enough to keep the cold, 5 degrees Celsius (41 degrees Fahrenheit) air out. The GIs were short on heating wood. The captives were hungry, and even with the few scratchy blankets they were provided, they were always cold.

The German youngsters were allowed to walk around somewhat freely within the perimeter of the camp, but GIs were everywhere, and armed soldiers were guarding each of the four corners of the closed off area, which was marked by a tank on each corner and two tanks along each of the four sides encircling the camp, along with a make-shift wired fence.

On this third day into captivity, Karl was roaming the grassy area near the food trucks, scavenging for leftover food. He found a few potato peels and carrot chunks in a large metal bucket used for collecting tossed away food scraps and other trash.

Karl carefully scanned the area to assure that nobody was watching him. When he felt safe, he bent down and grabbed the leftovers and then quickly switched between stuffing some of the food morsels into his pockets and others straight into his mouth. It all tasted bitter, but he would do anything to get rid of those hunger pangs. It was surprisingly a nice change from the bland soup broth and stale bread the GIs were feeding him. In the past few days, he had also been gathering nettle growing at the perimeter of the camp. He would pull the plant, hide it in his pocket, and then secretly eat it when nobody was looking. It tasted less bitter than the nettles they had found in the woods, so he decided that it would be a new supplement to his daily diet, whenever he could find it.

Out of the side of his eyes, Karl noticed a black GI passing by. Karl had never met a *Neger* (negro) in person until he had arrived at this American prison camp. Karl stopped his scavenging for a moment and nodded at him to say hi. He waited for him to pass and tracked the soldier out of the sides of his eyes. The black soldier then turned away, pretending not to notice, as Karl went back to digging through the trash for more scraps.

"Stop that!" Before Karl could finish his thought, a pock-faced Private at most five years older than him yanked him by his jacket collar away from the trash.

"Stop eating from the trash!" he slapped Karl's scraps right out of his hand. Karl chewed the rest of the potato peel and swallowed it as fast as he could. Karl pleaded with his eyes calmly with the young Private, with a name tag "Miller:" *"Ich bin sehr hungrig* (I am really hungry)," but piercing blue and determined eyes were staring back.

"Stop that! You could get sick from that!" Private Miller went on. Although Karl didn't speak any English, he got the point that the Private vehemently disapproved of his digging through the trash. "Get away from the trash!" he ordered again sternly. Then the Private let go of Karl's collar, but not before he shoved him in the direction he wanted him to go while he also waved his arm to chase Karl away as if to hush away a stray dog.

Karl adjusted his collar, tucked in his shoulders; put his hands in his pants pockets, and looked down and headed back toward his barracks building. Karl arrived back at his hall frustrated, deeply in thought and still hungry.

"Tomorrow we are starting work!" Frederick greeted him, lying in his bunk chewing on a piece of nettle. He also had picked up the habit of eating that bitter weed.

"What do you mean? What kind of work?" Karl was surprised. The seven days they had been here they hadn't been doing much. They had to clean out their own trash and keep their rooms cleaned, but other than that, one day after another had been a copy of the day before. Karl was getting the impressions that the GIs were trying to figure out what to do with all of these SS soldier boys, but they hadn't decided yet.

"They were looking for laborers, carpenters, and you told them you had been a carpenter apprentice right? They need carpenters. One of the sergeants was asking and I told him you...."

Before he could finish, a sergeant stepped inside the room, the same sergeant that Frederick must have been talking to. In broken German, he asked Karl: "Du bist Schreiner? (You are carpenter?) Wir brauchen dich morgen. (We need your help tomorrow!)"

Karl looked at the sergeant inquisitively and said, "Ja ich habe ein paar Jahre eine Schreinerlehre mitgemacht (Yes, I took part in a carpenter apprenticeship for a few years)."

That was more German than the sergeant could comprehend. He responded with repeating what he said before "Langsam! (Slow down.) Du bist Schreiner? (You are carpenter?)"

Karl shortened his response to make it easier to understand: “Ja, ich bin ein Schreiner!”

The sergeant’s face lit up at the confirmation. “Morgen wir dich holen. (Broken German: We will get you tomorrow.)”

Karl now put the tips of his fingers together and moved them back and forth from and to his mouth to motion he was hungry. He pleaded with the sergeant: “Ich habe Hunger! Ich kann so nicht arbeiten (I am too hungry, I can’t work like this).”

The sergeant surprisingly understood and responded with, “No worry, where you are going tomorrow there will be food. *Ja, essen morgen.”*

Karl was eager to find out where he was supposed to apply his carpentry skills and most importantly then where he finally would get more food. How much he longed for the feeling of a full stomach after one of his Mutter’s warm meals and for the first time in a long time he was looking forward to the next day. The thought of the unfinished desk for the Major ran through his mind: “*Did Mutter and Opa get it finished*?” He sure hoped so. He hadn’t thought about it for a while now, but that day he again shuddered just thinking about the multitude of possible consequences if the desk and chair weren’t done to spec and on time. The Major would take no excuses.

****

It was May 13, 1945 and it was sunny, but the air was crisp and cold. White clouds were hanging stark against the pale blue sky with the majestic grey mountains lining the horizon.

“Zum Tor, jetzt! (To the gate now!)” ordered Sgt. Fritz, in his deep thunderous voice as he moved his entire body and arms to point north to the gate, where a truck was sitting. It had been another cold night in the American prison camp. Today was the start of a new work detail for Karl and a few others. What exactly they would be doing and where they would be working was not yet clear to them.

Karl was the last one to climb out of his bunk and he raced out the barracks door toward the opening in the wire fence as fast as his long young legs could take him. Max, Wilfried, and Frederick, along with a few other German POWs had already lined up there. They were all waiting, heads down, with hands in their coat pockets, trying to use the small woolen space to keep their hands warm even though the rest of their bodies couldn’t seem to warm up. Karl was still wearing the same clothes he was given to by Lisl, covered by his “new” coat. The GIs had handed all of them scratchy woolen coats, some in better condition and better fitting than others. The steam of their breaths could be seen blowing in the cold mountain air.

Wilfried and Frederick were looking down, moving the grey stone gravel and dirt back and forth with their feet as if it were a contest. When he heard Karl approach, Max looked up, squinting against the rising sun, and gave Karl a slight nod. Wilfried and Frederick never looked up, their mind seemingly fiercely focused on the gravel game.

A truck was parked right next to one of the tanks that marked the internment camp’s border. As its driver started the engine the loud rattling motor disrupted the eerie silence of this fresh May morning. The smell of burning diesel filled the air.

Another sergeant, whom Karl hadn't seen before, was standing next to Sgt. Fritz in front of the truck holding his rifle over his shoulder. Karl read the sergeant's name tag: "Rotz." Karl was wondering whether Sgt. Rotz knew that his American name in German meant "snot" and he was slightly amused at the name, a reaction he was surprised to feel, as he hadn't felt it in a long time. He acknowledged again how relieved he was that the war was over and that he was with the Americans.

Karl was hungry, and his stomach lining felt like it was getting ready to digest itself. Why couldn't the GIs give them more to eat? He knew they also had little food and more food trucks were expected any day, but whenever the trucks got there, the GIs were the first ones to be fed, and the young POWs would get the only leftovers. Karl inhaled slightly as he saluted the soldiers.

Taking roll call and counting down, Sgt. Fritz yelled out the last names of the young captives one at a time:

"Schmidt!"

"Hier!" answered Max.

Fritz marked off Schmidt's name

"Elheusch!"

"Hier!" returned Karl.

Fritz checked off the names as one after the other responded with "Hier (here)"

Then Fritz yelled in German: "OK, we have the right guys here! I have all your names. Don't think we are not tracking you."

Sgt. Rotz ordered "Get on the back of the truck, now!" The young prisoners of war didn't need to understand English, they could read Rotz's body language: moving his rifle bud back and forth, he got them to quickly climb in the back of that truck. "Hurry! *Auf, auf! Schnell, schnell!"*

Karl was not sure what the big hurry was, but he and the other guys jumped up on the truck, filed in to the back. One by one they sat down on the cold floor of the cab and huddled close together. Even though the truck's cab was covered, the chilly mountain air was seeping through the cracks. Their grey and in some cases torn woolen winter coats didn't defend much against the morning cold even inside the truck.

After they were all piled in, Sgt. Rotz climbed onto the back of the truck and closed the hatch. He hollered, turning toward the cab of the truck, "All set!" loud enough for the driver to hear, and with a swift push to the pedal the truck rumbled off.

They were sitting quietly, wondering where they were being taken to on this fourth day of captivity, when burly Max leaned over to Karl and half-whispered — something that was almost impossible given Max's deep voice:

"Die Amerikaner haben Mauthausen vor ein paar Tagen befreit. Schrecklich! (The Americans liberated Mauthausen just a few days ago. It is a labor camp right outside Linz. They need a lot of help. Awful!)"

Everyone could hear him, and they all listened intensely, but nobody looked up or responded, too afraid to ask a question, heads down, with the question lingering in the air.

"When was he there? Why had he not talked about this yesterday when he got back?" Karl wondered. He had noticed though that usually obnoxious and loud Max had been quieter than usual last evening, but Karl had seen that as a welcome break and didn't want to question it.

They repeatedly rubbed their hands over their crossed arms up and down in hopes of generating some warmth. Karl was physically shivering.

The thought of innocent people being kept in these labor camps made the truck ride even colder, and Karl's teeth were now clattering from a combination of cold and worry. He now would have to face these prisoners but hopefully his youth would protect him from their potential wrath. What had Hitler done to this country? Karl now rubbed his hands up and down his arms, which had become even more muscular from digging trenches.

Max continued: "Thousands and thousands were killed.!"

"Killed? They killed the prisoners?! Only the worst offenders, right?"

Max answered: "They killed thousands! Prepare yourselves. They took a few of us to Mauthausen yesterday morning. I saw piles and piles of skeletons, dead after dead. You will see a lot of sick, cripples, half-deads. Hitler did a horrible thing. Hitler cheated us and he lied to us, all of us! And I am told there were many more camps.

Apparently Mauthausen was one of many camps to be liberated. The Russians have already liberated some others."

"Cripples!?" There was the mention again. Karl didn't want Hermann to be one of them there or in any camp.

"You there! Shut up! Halt's Maul! They'll see it soon enough!" ordered Sgt. Rotz, waving his rifle at Max.

Max stopped talking, leaned back and took a deep breath. Sgt. Rotz's German was surprisingly better than everyone had expected. He seemed to understand more than he could speak.

For the rest of the cold and bumpy twenty minute ride all remained silent, then suddenly Max pointed through one of the cracks in the back of the truck "*Look! Schau!*"

Karl turned around to look through the wide crack behind him. Their truck reached the end of one side of the wall and stopped at a grey stone gate. Karl noticed the carved out of rock "Nazi Eagle" sign on the ground – once no doubt hanging above the entrance – but now broken into two pieces laying on the side of the gravel road.

"The eagle was pulled off by the camp prisoners," Max whispered, ignoring Sgt. Rotz's earlier warning to stop talking.

The truck rattled through the gate as they all continued to peer through the cracks in the cab. There were a few people walking around inside the compound. Karl held his breath. What was this? He had to look really closely to make sure he knew what he was seeing: walking skeletons, just skin and bones, some their feet amputated with make-shift wooden sticks as feet, limping along with crutches, others just sitting and leaning against the building wall. All were wearing black and white striped pajama-like clothing.

Their truck then passed a rock quarry. Max whispered: “They made them break rocks,” and then he pointed to the stairs that lead up the quarry. “This was the ‘Todesstufe,’ the Stairs to Death. Here they forced prisoners to repeatedly carry heavy granite blocks up these stairs until they died, or they were murdered if they failed.”

“How do you know?” Frederick demanded.

“They told me this yesterday when I was here,” Max countered.

“Who told you?” Frederick continued his inquiry.

Sgt. Rotz leaned forward to face Frederick directly “He is right, that’s what *your* Hitler did!” he hissed at Frederick in his broken German.

Frederick immediately looked down, feeling guilty that he was associated with Hitler at all just by being German.

Nein, no that’s not possible, Karl thought, as everyone on the truck just stared ahead of them. Karl was aghast. Despite seeing some of the atrocities with his own eyes, he still couldn’t fully comprehend what he was witnessing.

They later learned that Max was right: the rock-quarry in Mauthausen was at the base of the infamous “Stairs of Death.” “Prisoners were forced to carry roughly-hewn blocks of stone — often weighing as much as 50 kilograms (110 pounds) — up the 186 stairs, one behind the other. As a result, many exhausted prisoners collapsed in front of the other prisoners in the line, and then fell on top of the other prisoners, creating a horrific domino effect; the first prisoner falling onto the next, and so on, all the way down the stairs. The concentration camp (KZ) Mauthausen was the only one in Austrian territory. At the time of the largest expansion, at the end of March 1945, it consisted of five different camps, each with 8,000 to 10,000 prisoners. In the Mauthausen camp, between 95,000 and 100,000 people were murdered: they starved or froze to death, died of disease or exhaustion; were beaten to death, shot while trying to flee, suffocated in the gas chambers, or died via heart injections or were otherwise executed." [vi]

Karl noticed the Red Cross flag blowing in the wind in place of where the Nazi flag undoubtedly hung just few days ago. The Red Cross organization had taken over managing the concentration camp (KZ). Together with the GIs and the help of young German prisoners of war (such as Karl, Frederick, Max and Wilfried) the Red Cross had begun the arduous task of cleaning up the KZ, burying the dead; and nursing the sick back to health before they could travel home. Where their homes were at this point was not immediately clear, since they had been corralled from all walks of life from all corners of Europe.

The truck came to a rumbling halt. With the rifle butt Sgt. Rotz nudged Max, who sat the closest to the exit. "Get down! *Runter!*" and he gestured for all of them to get off the truck. As soon as Karl jumped off, he was surrounded by a sweet odor in the air that burned his nose. He looked around and the eerie feeling that started in the truck was now overwhelming. All of a sudden he found it hard to breathe.

An older German civilian worker in worn-out blue overalls, hanging his head and looking grim, passed them, leading a horse by its halter. The horse was pulling a buggy full of stacked corpses. Karl looked on, holding his breath. He almost wanted to cover his eyes, but forced himself to look on in disbelief and bewilderment. At the other end of the building, two more civilian workers next to a stack of 40 or so bodies were grabbing corpses on each end — one the arms the other the legs — and swung them one by one onto another buggy hooked up to a plow horse with its head down, waiting. Flies were everywhere. Further up the north end of the KZ, civilian workers were digging graves for all these former prisoners who had died horrible deaths.

The stench was overpowering.

Karl pulled his dirty coat sleeve over his hand and then with it covered his mouth and nose, and not only to avoid the horrible smell. He wanted to wake up from this nightmare. His thoughts were racing. *What was this? What exactly happened here?*

At first he wanted to avoid it all and look away. Looking down he was starting to let it all sink in. He wanted it to not be true. He felt he had entered a horror show, a nightmare so unimaginable, something he didn't want to be part of. Hitler and his followers had lied to an entire country. Only the few closest to Hitler could have known what was really going on, Karl now told himself.

"We need you to help dig the graves and help bury these bodies!" Sgt. Rotz hissed at them, as if they had any responsibility in what happened here. "Spades are over there," he ordered and pointed in the direction of where the graves were being dug.

Karl bit his lips and clenched his fists. Tears were welling up in his eyes, but he forced them back. He tried to take a deep breath, but stopped because of the stench. He tried to block out what he was seeing and avoided any further thoughts of what had happened here. He just grabbed a spade and mechanically started digging alongside others: German civilians, GIs, young POWs, and even former KZ prisoners who were strong enough to help. As others already had started days before, they helped the next hours digging the graves.

Germans from Linz and the surrounding villages were already walking the KZ grounds; they had been ordered to come here to witness the atrocities and also to help clean up and dig the graves. Women with handkerchiefs in front of their faces walked by, many were crying, all looking solemn. A few threw up.

Buggy after buggy of piled up corpses were delivered to the trenches, and the bodies were dropped into the dug up, open earth. A GI eventually used a crawler tractor - Karl had never seen one before - to help move the bodies into the grave and to help push the dirt over the bodies.

That evening when Karl and the crew were brought back to his makeshift internment camp, nobody said a word. That night for the first time since the SS came to get him to join the war, Karl cried himself to sleep.

The next morning after being transported back to the KZ again, they were tasked again with helping to bury the bodies north of the camp. Then later that morning, when the boys again were near exhaustion and completely starved, Sgt. Rotz tapped Karl, Max, Frederick, and Wilfried on their shoulders.

"You are coming with me!"

Itching, dirty, fatigued and starting to feel his stomach turn again, Karl followed the group as first they leaned their spades against the wall of the building they were about to enter, then one by one, they piled into the front door of the first grey stone-building of the concentration camp. His eyes slowly adjusted to the dim light inside, and he tried to comprehend what he was seeing. On wooden bunk beds along the wall there were still hundreds of clothed skeletons. Or were they skeletons? They were moving – their heads were moving, staring at Karl directly through large dark hollowed eyes.

"You!" Sgt. Rotz addressed Karl and the rest of the young prisoners of war in his broken German: "Hier macht ihr genau was das Rote Kreuz euch befehlt. (Here you do exactly what the Red Cross personnel tell you to do.)" and reiterated in German. "They need your help, and these people here will give you the orders and you will follow them!" Karl examined the group of young men and women wearing clothes marked with the Red Cross insignia.

With his eyes fixed on the four young German prisoners of war, Sgt. Rotz continued pointing at the three Red Cross representatives just a few feet away, who were patiently waiting for Rotz to finish. "The Red Cross is in charge here. They are here to help the sick, to feed them, to clothes them, to heal and help them get better so they can go home! You are here to help the Red Cross with anything they need. Understood?!"

Two of the young prisoners of war nodded.

Sgt. Rotz was not happy with the slow, nonverbal response. He leaned in closer to them and screamed, specifically at Karl, who was still too shocked to react fast at all. "DO you understand?"

All of the prisoners then nodded and in almost unison, including Karl, they answered, *"Jawohl,* Sergeant!"

One of the Red Cross-badged guys now stepped forward and introduced himself, in a calm voice in fluent German:

"Ich heisse Marco Steiger (My name is Marco Steiger). Yes, we need a lot of help. You can help fix the bunks and chairs; you can help clean, cook, scrub. Some of the patients here have to be hand-fed, they are so weak they can't hold up their own bowls or spoons. They haven't had a full stomach in months or years. The nurses need help, the patients need to be fed slowly and given tiny amounts of food and drink at a time. The human waste bowls have to be emptied, there is a *Guelle* (liquid manure) where it all can be dumped in the back. We will show you where. Many of the concentration camp victims here are near death. We need to nurture them back to health. The ones that don't make it, need a deserving burial. The last few days we have sent the acutely ill patients to the Linzer hospital for special and critical care. More will need to be transported to the hospital today. Linzer is over capacity now. We have started to bring them to the hospital in the next town. Next

door, we've also set up a makeshift Lazarette (hospital) for the manageable and less urgent cases. Many are staying in their bunks until they get better; there is just not enough room for them all. The patients remaining here for treatment need to be made as comfortable as possible. Some of the bunks are stacked so closely we need to take out the middle layer to give the sick more space to move around, and the nurses need better access. We can use the extra wood for heat and cooking. Some of the bunks are broken or chipped, all need to be fixed; we don't want the sick to get hurt further. Typhus is rampant. Lice are everywhere; we need to scrub and scrub. When working here, wash your hands thoroughly and often. You don't want to catch Typhus!"

This was the first time in as long as Karl could remember that an adult had talked to him in a civil, respectful manner, without giving orders and simply treating Karl as an equal.

Marco's eyes were bloodshot. It was clear he hadn't slept much since he had arrived here. Passionately, he went on and on about their plans to get everyone back to health and out of there as fast as possible. Karl was impressed by Marco's demeanor and his determination was contagious. Karl was eager to help. "I have carpentry skills, I could help fix the bunks or chairs or anything you need fixed." Karl now knew specifically why he was here. The determination to help was masking the overpowering sickness he was feeling. For a moment he forgot his nausea and his hunger pains. He could help make these sick people be more comfortable. He was ready to roll up his sleeves and get to work. Whatever he could do to help here … to help them get better and get them back to their homes and families. Were their families left?

Sgt. Rotz angrily interrupted Karl and in his broken German he barked "Listen, Kraut! You do exactly what they tell you to do, whether that's cleaning out the shit from these sick people or carrying out the trash. You do what you are told!"

Karl wished that the sergeant could see that he just wanted to help, though he could somewhat empathize with the sergeant's resentment toward them, considering what his country had done. Sgt. Rotz vehemently hated anything German, or "Kraut" as he called them, and Karl could only imagine the horrible experiences he'd had, probably seen his comrades killed in combat and more.

"*I know I could help fix the bunks, I am good with wood,*" he defiantly thought, yet knew to remain quiet. Sgt. Rotz needed to calm down. None of the young POWs meant any harm, they were just young teenagers, hungry, tired and really just wanted to be in a warm bed at home with their families.

Marco completely ignored Sgt. Rotz's outburst and responded directly to Karl: "Oh that's good. We need carpentry skills. What's your name? *Wie heisst Du?*"

"Karl," was the quiet response, while carefully watching Sgt. Rotz's reaction out of the side of his eyes.

"Karl, why don't you go with Jim here," Marco instructed decisively while pointing at one of the other Red Cross workers standing next to him who appeared to be in his early 20s, "He can explain all the carpentry help that's needed and where the hammers and nails and other tools he found are, right Jim?"

Jim nodded as Marco continued in fluent German "I am told all four of you have carpentry skills, right?" he now addressed the rest of the team.

"You all could get started right away. There are many bunks to be fixed, and the middle bunks need taking down. We have more bunks than patients, removing some of the planks will give the sick more room. Some of the bunks are cracked: look at this one," he continued as he grabbed a nearby board that had come loose and easily lifted it up. "This is way too dangerous for anyone to sleep on, especially for the fragile sick that are here. Some of the boards have nails sticking out and just need to be hammered in. Some of the chairs' legs are wobbly and other repairs need to be made."

The men inspected the damaged furniture. After a short pause Marco repeated:

"The sick will be here for a while, at least until each is well enough so they can travel. We have to help them get better and make them comfortable in the meantime. And we can really use any extra wood for cooking and heating."

Jim tapped Max, Frederick and Wilfried on their shoulder: "All of you can now help with the wood work with me and Karl."

"You guys come with us," Jim said in his broken German, his brown eyes looked determined.

"What are your names?" he asked of his new crew.

They each respond.

"Max." "Frederick." "Wilfried."

"Follow me. Let me show you the tool shed we've uncovered." Jim marched ahead.

Sgt. Rotz started to tag along, stern and determined, but Marco stepped in between him and the assembled group and looked the sergeant firmly in the eyes. "Jim's got this, he can handle them! Robert here will take you to the kitchen. They need more help there with the food and cleanup. Can you get us some help there? Robert here will lead the way." Marco pointed to another one of the young Red Cross workers who had stepped forward. Robert was tall and blond, in his early twenties, with friendly blue eyes.

Sgt. Rotz hissed back, agitated. "Remember, they are all prisoners of war. They might try to run. You are now responsible for them!"

"Look at them, they are just kids, hungry and tired." Marco specifically pointed at Frederick, who in his oversized grey ripped coat and scrawny appearance looked more worried about his next meal than about escaping. "If it was for me, they wouldn't even be here, I'd send them back home. But I respect that you captured them as prisoners of war, but don't expect me to treat them badly! I'll use their help, but that is it!" There was clear disagreement between the soldier and the Red Cross worker as to how these teenagers should be treated. "...and where would they run to anyhow? There is nothing for miles and miles, with the Russians on the other side." Marco now was really annoyed with Sgt. Rotz.

Rotz just motioned at the young captives with his rifle, ignoring Marco's outburst: "Just go," he ordered them with an irritated voice. "Remember, all of you meet back at the truck exactly at 19:00."
"Yes, sir!" the prisoners responded.
With that, Jim who had just stood there watching the heated exchange between Marco and Sgt. Rotz, slowly motioned to Karl and the rest of the group and said. "Alright, we all heard what the sergeant said. We will have you ready and back to him by 19:00. Let's go!"
With that, Jim walked off with Karl, Max, Frederick and Wilfried in tow.
Robert brought Sgt. Rotz to the kitchen, while Marco went off to check on the other Red Cross workers. He had to welcome and coordinate other batches of helpers.
Jim and his newly formed crew walked through the connected grey and dark buildings, only a few electric bulbs lighting up the hallways. Bunk after bunk covered the walls, with the skeletons on them, people just skin and bones, some laying down and resting, others actually with their heads in their hands watching the new arrivals.
"Water, please," a weak voice pleaded. It was one of the *Kranken* (sick), as Karl called the former *KZ-Haeftlinge* (camp prisoners). "I am so thirsty."
It was an older patient, trying to sit up, his age was hard to judge as he was very malnourished. Karl guessed him at 50. Jim walked over to tell him that the nurse would be back around soon again with

more water. The man laid back down. Karl didn't even want to dare to ask nor think about what that man had been through.

They moved on passed many more patients and then they heard another younger, whiny voice pleading "Water, please, I really need water. I have a bad headache." Jim slowly walked over to check on the desperate sounding youngster. He gently touched the malnourished kid's leg. "They will come around shortly and bring water and food for everyone. You had water less than an hour ago, right?"

The sick boy barely nodded. He looked so malnourished that Karl wasn't sure why he hadn't been one of the sick who were transported to the hospital.

Karl looked closer; there was something about him that looked familiar. Was it...? Could it be…?

"Michael?" It couldn't be! The light was dim, and shadows were falling over the barely alive skeleton. His facial features were almost unrecognizable. The boy reacted slowly; his eyes, though open, seemed dead.

"You know him?" Jim looked at Karl inquisitively.

"I think so." Karl responded nodding, continuing to stare at the Kranken, to study him more.

Jim now leaned in even closer to the boy and slowly picked up his bony hand to stroke it. Touching this boy or any of the Kranken was dangerous because any of them could have a contagious disease such as typhus, tuberculosis, and others. Many had lice.

Jim in his broken German continued to calm the boy: "You can't drink too much at once; your body has to get adjusted slowly. They will be back shortly with more water and food. You gradually have to start eating and drinking again, otherwise you will get very sick or you could even die." Jim again pointed at the danger of eating or drinking too much at once, when the body was not used to it.

Jim stroked the Kranken's hand a few more times, then slowly put it back down on the wooden plank.

Jim moved back, and Karl took a step forward towards the Kranken.

"Michael?" he questioned, leaning down towards him. He was now almost certain it was Michael, the kid from their neighborhood he and Hans used to play with, and who was there the day Albert cut Karl at the creek. Their adventurous times together were now flashing through Karl's mind. Soccer games behind their house, with makeshift goals, and many races run through forbidden wheat-fields, Michael helping out with all their chores, cutting trees and planting potatoes. Karl had been so busy with his own tumultuous life that he hadn't thought about Michael lately, but now all his childhood memories with Michael were vivid.

He was barely recognizable, half his weight, with sunken dead eyes, no hair. Was it completely shaven, or had his hair fallen out from malnutrition?

Michael looked at Karl, and as if finally recognizing him, his eyes attempted to smile weakly: "Karl," he muttered barely. And then again "Karl!" The surprise in his voice was clear.

"Michael, I am here! I am here to help you. I will help make you better. I am so sorry!" Karl now grabbed Michael's hand and held it, tears again welled up in Karl's eyes. What did Michael have to endure here? Now it was all falling into place. Michael Morgenthau was the son of the only Jewish family in their neighborhood; whose family's only small jewelry store in their entire small village had been boarded up and shut down by the Nazis. Karl remembered how Mutter had always wished she could afford anything in that store, the jewelry was beautiful, and she loved going there just to look and dream about having that one specific white pearl bracelet. On the 10th anniversary of Karl's father's death, Opa had surprised Mutter with that same bracelet as a gift. At first, Mutter scolded him for splurging so much, when they had so little, but Opa had assured her that he had just built a chest of drawers for the Morgenthau's in return. The Morgenthau's were good people.

Karl remembered how upset his Opa and Mutter were when the store was shuttered down with a huge Star of David painted on it along with a "Closed" sign. He remembered when Mutter had whispered about their arrest at Michael's grandparents' house and how they had just vanished.

"So this is where they took you." Karl now understood why nobody could have known where the Nazis had taken them. Nobody in his village knew about Mauthausen. The grizzly puzzle was starting to fit together.

Jim stepped back in, continuing to try to help calm Michael: "We have to fix some of the bunks, Karl has work to do, but my other colleagues will be around soon, I'll make sure of that. If I come back around and you still don't have water, I'll personally get you some, OK?"

The sick boy seemed to be comforted and slowly laid his slightly lifted head back down.

"Karl," Michael repeated one last time.

"What?" Karl responded holding his breath.

"Mom and Dad and my sister Anna are all dead! They were all killed here!" Michael barely managed to say. His eyes looked cold and stared straight up at the ceiling.

"Mein Gott! Wie schrecklich! (My god, how horrible!)" Karl whispered, trying to lean back over Michael, but that was his only response. He kept his real feelings inside. Karl really just wanted to scream at this point. All the anger of the past months was culminating at that moment.

Controlling every nerve and emotion his body wanted to emit, Karl leaned forward again and promised: "Michael, I won't ask any questions right now. Don't think about it now. Think about getting better; focus on yourself. You need to carry on the family legacy. I will make sure they take good care of you. You are now safe and in good hands. You are with the Americans, they will take care of you. Hitler killed himself. The war in Germany is over. They will get you better, and I'll make sure of that. Before you know it, you'll be back home. You will be out of here before me, and then please say hi to Mutter for me." Karl's words were just pouring out of him, and he firmly believed that Michael would be home before him. Who knew if Karl would ever see home again.

"We need to keep going!" Jim now broke off the unlikely reunion. It was bittersweet and Jim could hardly believe these two strangers knew each other. But they all had a lot of work to do. Many more needed help here.

Karl gently squeezed Michael's hand one final time and said, "Bis bald! ("See you soon!)" and leaned forward for a light hug, realizing Michael was too weak to be grabbed.

"Don't!" Jim freaked out. "Don't hug him! You don't want to get sick!" With that Jim walked off.

Karl followed Jim and the rest of the crew, who had been standing there watching the interaction in amazement.

Jim continued down the hall, but Karl caught up and tapped Jim's shoulder. "Could I get him and us some water? Could we also get him another blanket? He seems so cold!" Jim turned around and studied Karl's face, recognizing the worried but determined look. Then looking toward Michael again behind them, Jim nodded his approval and pointed Karl in the direction of the former SS kitchen. Karl ran towards it where he found armed guards huddling in the kitchen. Karl saw a water canister but didn't dare to take it.

"Who are you with? Where is your group?" one of the GIs in the kitchen immediately grabbed Karl's underarm.

"He is with me!" Jim knew to follow Karl because he would not be allowed to roam alone without supervision. He was also worried about Sgt. Rotz's temper from the little interaction he had with him.

The soldier looked at Jim, and before he let go of his grip Karl yanked himself loose; he was getting tired of being treated like a criminal; he just wanted to help. He didn't understand exactly what they were saying, but it clearly sounded angry. Then he realized that Jim told the soldier that all was fine.

The armed GI continued to explain himself to Jim, as if he felt bad that he was mean to Karl: "We found a load of stored potatoes the SS had been hoarding. They let the prisoners starve but had months' worth of potatoes here. We are guarding the supply because some of the former prisoners might come here and try to steal the potatoes, eating themselves to death. They have to eat slowly until their bodies get used to food again, we are told. So I am here to guard all the food!"

"Oh, I know they are eager to eat, we would be too! Some haven't had a full meal in years. Good to hear about this large potato supply. And we also have our military rations, so we are good. For now we just need some water." Jim replied.

The GI pointed to the faucet and water canisters and nodded his approval to Karl. Karl filled up a canister, and carrying it, he ran back to Michael and handed it to him. 'No!' Jim grabbed the canister of water back, "He can only sip this. Remember, he will get really sick if he drinks too much or too fast, or he could even die. Let me run and grab a cup from the kitchen." With that Jim ran off and within minutes came back cup in hand.

He turned to Michael. "Take it slow. Your body is not used to this." Karl then slowly lifted up Michael's head and let him take a small slow sip from the filled cup. Some of the water spilled down Michael's face and neck. Karl quickly wiped it off with his coat sleeve.

Michael's deep-set eyes looked at Karl with so much warmth and appreciation that no words would have been able to express more thanks.

At that moment, Karl felt closer to Michael than he ever had before, even while growing up and playing together in the same neighborhood. Back then they took each other for granted and they were carefree, never questioning their freedom. Now they were reconnected both having survived the war thus far in their own tragic ways. Karl realized that in comparison the path his fate had taken him was much smoother than Michael's, who had been tortured here and had lost his family. Michael, 17 and only one year older than Karl, had aged many years physically by that horrendous treatment and now his body was ravaged by starvation and disease. The emotional effect of all of that happened to him was not even comprehensible. Karl there and then recognized that in comparison he could not complain about his fate any longer, if only he knew his family was still alive.

"Don't you think a nurse should look at him?" Karl asked Jim, concerned. Now that he had found his friend, he didn't want to lose him again. "Could we find one of those Red Cross nurses I had seen walking around earlier. They need to diagnose him."

Karl felt responsible for ensuring Michael's recovery. "*How could they not have found a way to hide this family in their village*?" Karl asked himself for a moment, but immediately knew the answer. "*First, nobody really expected the Morgenthau family would be arrested and brought here. No one in his village knew these camps existed. Second in a small village it was nearly impossible to hide anyone. They all could have ended up here*!"

"As mentioned, the critically ill have already been transported to the hospital. That means Michael has already been examined. He will be fine. A few more weeks here and he will be good as new." Jim winked at Karl, trying to lighten the mood in one of the saddest situations Karl had ever found himself in.

Jim was now eager to move on. He knew he couldn't get bogged down by one patient. There was too much to do, too many needed their help. "Let's go now, we have work to do!" With that, the young POWs followed him again, leaving Michael behind along with the many other patients, young and old, some in better health than others. They walked in and out of buildings; they passed a double crematory oven in the underground area between the hospital building and the bunker. They later found out that this oven had been installed just a few weeks before the KZ camp had been liberated. The ovens were originally designed as baking ovens; surely the makers of these ovens couldn't have imagined what they eventually would be used for. Some of the buildings were labeled "Shower Rooms." Jim stopped and pointed at them. In his broken German, he explained in a somber voice: "Here was where the Nazis killed thousands. These "shower rooms" were actually Zyklon-B gas chambers. People were initially lured into these rooms thinking they would shower but instead they all were all brutally gassed. After a while, people had figured out that they weren't showers, but knew that resistance was impossible. Thousands were gassed in here. If you didn't go along, you would be tortured to death. Gassing was the quicker and less painful option."

Jim looked down and folded his hands in front of him, as if to take a moment and pay respect in memory of the atrocities and all the innocent killed here. The young German prisoners now also looked down. Karl again had that churning stomach feeling, and he now felt he had to throw up. The fatigue and digesting all he was seeing was mentally and physically just getting to be too much.

Jim was grasping the door handle to one of the "shower" rooms but then noticed that Karl's face matched the color of the grey walls: "Are you alright? You don't look too good."

Karl felt his knees collapse and held on to each to stabilize his body with both hands. His head nearly between his knees, he weakly tried to assure Jim "I am fine!"

Comforting Jim put his hand on Karl's shoulder.

"You are going to be fine! These were horrible atrocities Hitler and the Nazis have committed. You are too young; you could not have stopped anything. There was not much you four could have done, and if you would have tried you would have ended up in here or in one of the many other concentration camps throughout Europe I am hearing about that have been uncovered. Mauthausen is hopefully one of the last camps to be liberated!" Jim was trying to console the teenagers.

Frederick was leaning against the wall, silently crying, tears running down his face. Then he lowered himself, crumbling against the wall, and cried so hard his entire body shook, then he wrapped his arms around his knees and buried his head in them. Max put his hand on Frederick's shoulder trying to console him, while he also wiped some tears with his sleeves. Out of the group of four, Max seemed to have himself most under control.

Jim still had his hand on Karl's shoulder, while Wilfried grabbed Karl's arm to try to help him stand up straight again. No one said a word.

"Follow me, let's just go outside for a minute and get some fresh air." With that, Jim led them to the nearest door to take them outside. The much-sought-after relief outside did not come for Karl. Instead he felt he could smell the stench of burned and dead bodies in the air, just as when he first got here. The crematorium ovens had been out of service only a few days. The creepy sweet stench was still lingering. The thin mountain air was trying to seep through and filter out what was left in the air of the horrible tragedy, but it would take months before the air was semi-pure and somewhat fresh again.

Karl avoided taking deep breaths. The thought of particles of burned flesh still in the air revolted him. Karl's body heaved, and he took a few steps forward into the middle of the gravel road and then threw up uncontrollably. Because he had eaten so little for so long, he just kept gagging and throwing up green liquid bile. The raw nettles were making their way back up. When nothing was left to throw up, he dry-heaved and finally wiped his face with his sleeve and then just let himself fall down; he lay there in the collapsed fetal position. His entire experience, from the time they were taken in the middle of the night, to digging the trenches, to being commanded to the front to now and the unbelievable things he was witnessing, was more than the young man could handle. Karl sobbed uncontrollably.

Max tried to walk toward Karl, but Jim motioned as if to say it might be best for Karl to be left alone and to just let it all out.

All the pain Karl had felt, all the fear and the emotions he had held in since the night the SS came to get them from Mutter's house was then being released. Most of all, Karl couldn't believe how much he and his country had been deceived by the tyrant Hitler and his blind followers, the Nazis. *"Was a concentration camp where his brother Hermann ended up? Where was his brother Hans? Was he still alive? Was he in a Russian prison camp somewhere? Was he being tortured? How was his Mutter doing? His Opa? Did the Russians leave them be? Where was his uncle? How could he be from a country that was run by this tyrant and murderer?"* He was overcome with shame. Karl let it sink in for the first time how the war had torn his entire family and his young life apart. Germany was in ruins.

Max, Wilfried, and Frederick just sat crisscrossed around Karl, all hung their heads low and thought their own worried thoughts, using their sleeves to wipe their tears here and there.

Karl eventually stopped crying, but laid there still overcome with worry and anxiety. He now turned his head up and looked into the sky as if his green eyes were asking: *"How could you let this happen?"*

Even though Jim was part of the team of liberators, he empathized with the boys. He started to explain all that he knew about the background in his broken German. "The Nazis killed Jews and anyone trying to fight the regime. I am hearing, that they put them in camps like these all over Europe. Hitler wrote in his book *Mein Kampf* about his hatred for the Jews. He blamed the Jews for signing the World War I treaty that heavily favored the enemies and ruined the German economy."

Karl looked up at Jim while still lying on the ground, shielding his eyes from the red and pink sun that was now setting behind Jim's head. Karl appreciated the fact that this American knew what Hitler wrote in *Mein Kampf.*

Lifting his head, Karl responded slowly in his best High German to make it easier for Jim to understand, because Jim would have an impossible time comprehending Karl's Southern German Bavarian dialect.

"Richtig! (Right!) We were in the Hitler Jugend. It was required of all teenagers to be part of the Hitler Jugend. *Mein Kampf* was required reading. We discussed it at length at many of the Hitler Jugend meetings. Yet, we didn't know that Hitler actually was burning humans to death. That was never discussed. How sick, how mentally deranged?" Karl put his head back down slowly but at this point he was all cried out. The reality of all of it had sunk in, and he realized he needed to pick himself up now again and move on.

Jim was more understanding and patient than probably any GI would have been. Here they were from two opposing countries — enemies in the war — talking and debating war crimes as if they were friends. Jim himself wasn't too much older than these teenagers and luckily for the boys was very sympathetic to their plight, but he also knew how much work there was to get done.

Karl sat up. He looked over and noticed a pile of paper sacks laying against the wall of one of the grey KZ buildings. Jim followed his glance and pointed out that those paper bags also had been used to dispose the dead bodies. Karl quickly looked away, he didn't want to get started again.

"We'd better go before Sgt. Rotz sees you sitting here! We are here to help the survivors. We need to nourish them and get them better and make them feel comfortable while they are healing. They are still dying by the dozens daily. The way you could make a difference now is to help the helpers, who are trying to make these people better as fast as possible and get them back on their feet! Let's fix the furniture, let's fix the bunks, give the sick what they need, scrub everything. Let's make it as livable here as possible."

Karl slowly got himself up. Using his sleeve, he wiped away his last few tears and then straightened out his torn coat. Max, Frederick and Wilfried then followed Jim inside, and Karl slowly joined them. On the way in, Karl noticed the large blackened chimney of the crematorium. He stared at it for a second, then shook his head. He just continued to follow the group back into the buildings. No, he didn't want to think about it all for another minute; he knew he would get sick again. He needed to stay healthy to be able to help. He didn't want to also become a burden. He couldn't even fathom the type of people who blindly followed these orders to kill hundreds and thousands this way. How mentally sick and brainwashed and possibly even scared they themselves must had been. How did they justify this to themselves? How could they go home to their families? What would they tell them at the end of a work day, if anything?

The group followed Jim until he stopped in front of a large majestic oak closet; Karl fleetingly admired the excellent carpentry work of the chiseled floral design on its cover. The keys were in its doors and Jim unlocked and opened them. Neatly lined up in it were saws, hammers, screwdrivers, hundreds of different sized nails and screws, from small to large, thin to thick and anything one would need for fixing these bunks, chairs and other furniture.

Karl was able to gain control over his feelings. His focus shifted to help out and get the Kranken (sick) healthy again. Karl's determination to support the healing and help out as much as possible was renewed. He felt he had a purpose!

With the teenaged boys in tow, Jim walked back through the barracks and pointed at more bunks that needed to have boards removed.The nurses would literally have to crouch down and nearly crawl or climb on top of the bunks to get to some of the patients.

The guys now quickly got to work. There was so much to be done and enough work for all four that it could take weeks to complete. They began to hammer and saw away at the bunks. They completed one bunk after the other, and then moved on to the next. "*I wonder how long it will take to get everyone healthy here; how long will it take to clean up?*" Karl again was wondering whether he'd ever see home again.

"Karl?" Karl stopped sawing to look up and noticed Michael right there. Karl hadn't realized they had come back to the same area they had left him at before; they came in through a different door, and all of the bunks looked the same in the dim lighting. Karl was now finding his bearings. He had been deep in thought, sawing away.

"Ja, Michael?"

Karl knew he was supposed to work, but didn't see any harm in responding to Michael.

"Where is Hans?"

Karl stopped for a second before he responded, "I don't know, Michael."

"What about Hermann?"

"I am not sure!"

"Did you ever hear from your Uncle Joseph again?"

"No, nothing!"

"How are your Mutter and Opa?"

"I think they are at home, but I am not sure, I haven't seen them since October last year."

"What months is it now?"

"It's May, 1945, Michael."

Michael just stared, his face empty of emotions.

"Michael, it's probably best if you rest now and don't talk that much. I also have to work. I am an American prisoner of war. I surrendered to the GIs because I didn't want to be captured by the Russians. There is so much more I want to tell you, but it will have to be later. I have to work or I will get in trouble — I won't be able to hear you when I start sawing again, OK?" With that, Karl continued his work. It was Karl's way of blocking away the pain he felt now for Michael and his family and for himself and not knowing about his brothers, Mutter, Opa, uncle Joseph, and all the others who suffered or died here.

Using his arms behind his head to prop it up, Michael watched Karl saw away, too weak to sit up.

"How are you a POW? You are too young to be a soldier!"

Karl didn't want to explain too much at that point to not upset Michael.

Karl avoided eye contact: "I had no choice. But you need to rest, Michael! We'll talk later when you feel better and are stronger. I'll be back here tomorrow. Every day here you will get better and stronger."

Karl now busily continued to saw at the board on the middle bunk right over next to Michael's bunk. Max joined Karl, pulling in tandem on the other end of the saw, and once finished sawing, together they carried the boards out after they were sawed off. They made a wood pile outside, since they wanted to use it as fire wood. They sawed and evened out some of the uneven posts and sanded down others.

“We now need you to take these buckets and fill with water and soap. The Red Cross needs help with cleaning the bunks; each one in here needs to be scrubbed down. Here take these rags.” Jim directed Wilfried, handing him a metal bucket and a rag. “Once you are done scrubbing bunks, the nurses need help washing the patients!”

Karl and Max spent the rest of the day hammering, sawing, moving wooden boards and repeating the tasks bunk after bunk. “*How much pain these bunks have seen, how much suffering and death. How many died in these bunks*?” Karl didn’t want to think about it anymore, ignoring the blood splattered on some of the boards, he kept hammering and sawing, sweat pouring down his face and body. Then, when the sun started to set, they were told it was time to go back. At exactly 19:00, Jim led them to the idling truck by the gate. Sgt. Rotz already impatiently stood outside, waiting to take his POWs back to their internment camps for the night.

Exhausted and back in their barracks the boys were fed watery soup and dried bread, and shortly afterwards they went back to their rooms to sleep. Nobody spoke as all were lost in their own thoughts.

The next day they were again shuttled back to the concentration camp (KZ). Jim handed them buckets and directed them towards the water and soap in the former prisoner kitchen. That day, more help was needed to scrub the quarters and further disinfect everything. Karl took a rag and dipped it into the scalding hot water - his hands almost burned. They really needed to use the hottest water and the only soap available. Karl wrung out the suds of the rag and started to wipe down bunk after bunk. "*I wonder if the prisoners had cleaned the bunks up until then, but after a while they all were too weak to clean and the captives must not have cared. That's how the diseases started.*" Karl couldn't even image the day to day activities of a prisoner here, before they were liberated. "*How could they even sleep after a hard day's work in the rock quarry, with hardly any food in their stomach, and all that worry about dying any day? The worry alone must have been torture! Did they become too weak to care after a while?*" Karl kept scrubbing and scrubbing bunk after bunk, with his thoughts racing.

Some of the Kranken gave Karl a smile of thanks, others who felt stronger, patted him on the back. Karl really enjoyed doing this work, and he felt he was finally somewhat useful.

After they were done scrubbing down the bunks, Jim told Karl and Max he needed again help to continue fixing the bunks. There was an endless list of tasks to be completed.

At one point after a few weeks, the GIs realized that they were losing the fight against the various diseases, and they decided the only way to contain them further was to burn down some of the still infected smaller camps. All the cleaning hadn't helped, and Typhus and tuberculosis just couldn't be eradicated. The Kranken were still dying daily.

A few camp buildings were then burned down using a controlled fire and Karl was a bit discouraged that all their scrubbing, fixing and working on the bunks in those buildings had been in vain.

The remaining camps had to be then sterilized more thoroughly than before. Together with other German civilians who were ordered here daily to help, the four cleaned and scrubbed and when the nurses needed more help with the "sick" they cleaned out bedpans and helped wash, clean, and feed all the Kranken. Often when cleaning them, Karl had to carefully dab around their scabs and wounds. "*I don't even want to know how he's got them!*" Karl often thought, he avoided the questions and remained cheerful with each of them – he knew he couldn't handle the explanations as to how they each got their scars and often still open wounds.

Their daily tasks started to become routine. Karl made it a point each day to stop by and visit Michael just for a few minutes; more wasn't allowed; they were ordered here to work and not to socialize, Sgt. Rotz had made that clear. Karl always made sure Michael had enough water, enough food, and made sure to give him anything he needed. If Michael felt cold, Karl ran off to get him more blankets and made sure the doors were closed to keep the cool air out. If he was hot, Karl ran to open the door to let fresh air in. A few times they reminisced about the good times in their neighborhood growing up together. Of course Karl couldn't give Michael back his family, which was what he would have needed most to heal faster. Karl completely avoided that topic, and didn't bring up what happened to Albert, their one time childhood friend and turned SS fanatic. Karl also didn't talk about his worries about his own family. He wanted Michael to focus on the positives and the now to help him heal. Later, once Michael was stronger again, there would be plenty of time to go into those traumatic details, if needed. Though in reality, Karl would not talk about his experience in Mauthausen for the next 20 years.

The immediate goal was to just get Michael healthy.

At the end of the first week, Michael was able to sit up on his own. With the help of a Red Cross nurse he even took a couple of steps. Michael seemed to be on his way to recovery. On the following Wednesday, to Karl's surprise, Michael smiled bigger than usual at him and whispered: "Komm naeher (Come closer)." And when Karl curiously leaned in, Michael slowly pulled out a chocolate bar from behind his back. Karl laughed so hard, he thought Michael was like a magician pulling a rabbit out of his hat. That moment Karl realized that it was great to be able to laugh again.

"Here I've saved this for you," Michael proudly handed the chocolate to Karl, with the biggest grin Karl had seen on Michael since they were reunited.

"Chocolate!" Karl read the label. "Schokolade!" and grabbed the desired sweets. "Oh danke, Michael, danke! I haven't eaten chocolate in years."

"Hide it!"

"I will," and Karl shoved the bar into this coat pocket, looking around and making sure that nobody had seen this interaction. A few of the Kranken might have seen it, but if they did they had looked away and didn't say anything. Shortly after, barely able to contain his excitement, Karl snuck into the KZ bathroom and inside the stall savored that treat. He let the chocolate melt in his mouth. He didn't want anyone else to see or possibly envy his bounty. He certainly didn't want to share this first chocolate bar he had eaten in years.

Though Karl had to overcome his disgust for working in the concentration camp environment and all it stood for - and also cleaning out the messy bed pans and vomit often made his stomach turn - he then started to look forward to his daily visit with Michael, his only connection to home. Michael now always saved chocolate bars and other treats for Karl. The news of the liberation of this yet another horrid camp had spread, and the food trucks were supplying the KZ with much needed nourishment for the Kranken on a regular basis. They also had to know that chocolate made anyone happier, and a happy person heals faster, Karl was certain.

As every day then, Karl and the other guys piled onto the truck idling ready in front of the internment camp each morning and Sgt. Rotz eagerly delivered them to Jim. Daily the boys were immediately put to work and eagerly completed any tasks assigned. One or the other was always seen with a bucket of soap water. They could never clean enough, and the bunks got wiped down daily. They continued to wash down the Kranken who still couldn't shower. Cleanliness to fight the diseases was still one of the biggest challenges. The spread of disease needed to be contained.

Hunger was no longer an issue for the boys. Sgt. Fritz had been right, when he first told Karl about the assignment. The Kranken were being fed well by the Red Cross with the potato stash that had been uncovered and the various food supplies that were pouring in, and in turn the Kranken sneaked chocolate and crackers and other food to the boys, for whom they were so thankful for helping them get better; whether it was cleaning out their bedpans, helping them to the bathroom, shower, or bringing them cooked meals. They were thankful for everything these young boys did for them.

Hunger though was still a huge problem for his German POW mates back at the internment camp. Karl wished he could take back some of the extra food to their internment where some of his camp mates were left behind, still hungry, but he was not allowed to take any food supplies back with them. At the end of each work day at the concentration camp (KZ), Karl and his comrades were searched before being taken back, to make sure they were not bringing back any food. The concern was that food from the KZ could also be contaminated and carried some of the diseases rampant there and spread it to the barracks where the rest of the German POWs were being held.

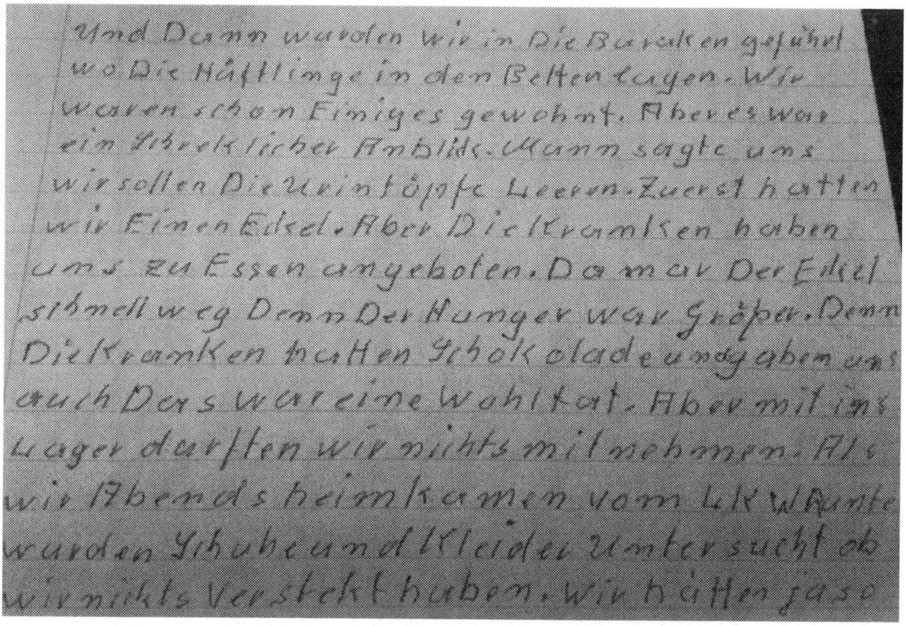
Und Dann wurden wir in Die Baracken geführt
wo Die Häftlinge in den Betten lagen. Wir
waren schon Einiges gewohnt. Aber es war
ein schrecklicher Anblick. Mann sagte uns
wir sollen Die Urintöpfe Leeren. Zuerst hatten
wir Einen Ekel. Aber Die Kranken haben
uns zu Essen angeboten. Da war Der Ekel
schnell weg Denn Der Hunger war Größer. Denn
Die Kranken hatten Schokolade und gaben uns
auch Das war eine Wohltat. Aber mit ins
Lager durften wir nichts mitnehmen. Als
wir Abends heimkamen vom LKW Runter
wurden Schuhe und Kleider Untersucht ob
wir nichts Versteckt haben. Wir hätten ja so

Karl was immensely thankful for his job: using his carpentry skills he could make the Kranken feel more comfortable and get better, also gone were the daily hunger pangs. He also could personally tend to his childhood friend. What were the chances of him finding Michael here? It must have been a sign of good things to come.

Michael one day told him about how he witnessed a few cripples being euthanized here, their only "crime" had been that they were handicapped, and he cried about how horrible it was to watch these helpless being killed.

"Sssshhhhhh!" Karl put his finger to his lips. "Please, for now, let's not talk about it anymore!"

Karl had heard and seen enough of the unspeakable gruesomeness. Hearing about the cripples, he couldn't help but worry even more about the whereabouts of Hermann, and of course Hans, Mutter, Opa and his uncle. Would he ever see them again?

With the constant worry at the back of his mind, he continued his daily labor. Today an unusual itch slowed him down. It was an itch that just didn't want to stop: first his head, then his arms.

Lice!

He then itched all over and scratched himself non-stop. Nobody was really surprised when Karl also got lice, because most everyone already had them.

"Don't scratch, it won't help!" Jim advised. It was difficult not to scratch, and back at the internment camp that night Karl could not sleep at all, as the pain kept him awake. The next day, back at the concentration camp, he asked a Red Cross nurse for advice on what to do about the lice, but he didn't get a good answer.

Karl had an idea. He recalled all the large paper sacks that were lying around against the KZ walls which had originally been used for disposing the dead bodies; that day he tracked them down and decided to sleep in nothing but one of these "body" sacks each night. While it didn't contribute any warmth, it helped keep the lice that were nesting in his clothes away. Despite hand-washing all the clothes, it was impossible to quickly get rid of them. They had nested in his hair and in his clothes.

Karl showered and scrubbed himself more than ever; he then requested a razor from Jim to shave his head completely bald. Watching his red curly hair drop on the floor, he hoped to get rid of the pest. Like wildfire, the lice spread and before too long all his roommates at the internment also had them. How fast they spread! The roommates requested he bring them back some of these paper bags and Karl got approval from Jim to take more back to the POW camp and the rest of his roommates also started to sleep in them. The thought that these paper bags were reserved for corpses was pushed aside quickly.

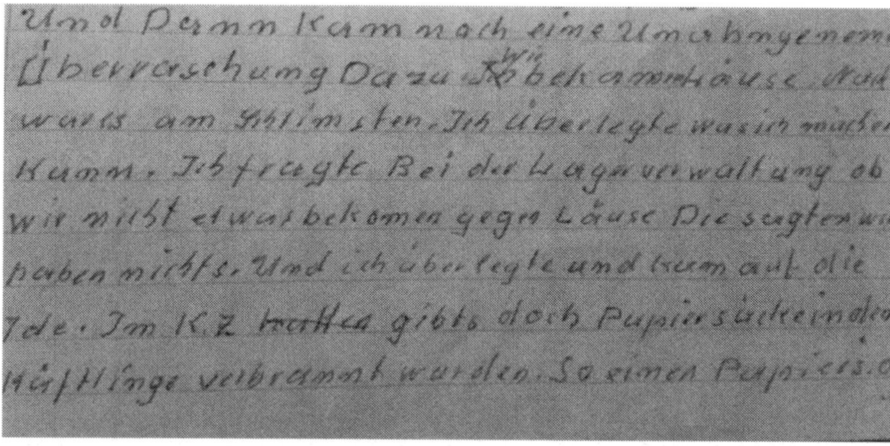
Und Dann Kam noch eine Unangenehme
Überraschung Dazu wir bekammen Läuse Nach
wars am Schlimsten. Ich überlegte was ich machen
Kann. Ich fragte Bei der Lagerverwaltung ob
wir nicht etwas bekomen gegen Läuse Die sagten wir
haben nichts. Und ich überlegte und kam auf die
Idee. Im K.Z hatten gibts doch Papiersäcke in den
Häftlinge verbrannt wurden. So einen Papiersä

The lice again had kept him scratching every inch of his body during his 30th night in American "captivity." Again he barely got any sleep – lice crawling all over. In the early day light the next morning, before getting ready for yet another truck ride to the concentration camp, he could see he had red blotches all over his arms and legs. He was tired and cold, his bald head was itching and his skin was burning. He rushed over to grab his clothes and got dressed as fast as he could, testing his self-control by not scratching; knowing it would make the itching only worse. Karl again was the last one to get to the truck.

When he arrived at the concentration camp, as it was now his daily routine , he headed straight for Michael's bunk. When he got there, to his surprise today Michael's bunk was completely cleaned out with not even a blanket on it. Karl was baffled. "*Where could Michael be? Were his blankets and pillow being washed? Was Michael at the latrine or showering?*"

Michael had regained much of his strength and by then could move around on his own, though he still needed a cane. When Karl checked back on him a few minutes later, he was still not back.

A worried feeling overcame him. "*What happened to Michael? He seemed healthy yesterday morning!*" That's when he last had seen Michael. By now they were allowed to walk through the KZ on their own and Karl found Jim: "Could you find out where Michael is?"

"Sure," Jim and Karl walked back to near Michael's bunk and Jim called over one of the young blond Red Cross nurses who happened to walk by, ready for her shift.

"The guy that was in this bunk bed over there, the young kid named Michael, do you know where he is?"

The exhausted looking nurse thought for a minute, then blew her blond bangs out of her face "Yes, Michael. Late last night he came down with a really bad fever. They suspected Typhus, and they immediately transported him to the hospital in Linz."

"Typhus?" Karl was baffled. "But he was feeling better!"

Chapter 9

Ruins

From that day on, Karl began searching for Michael. His continued attempts to track Michael down failed. Day after day he pleaded with Jim to drive him or even let him walk the 5 kilometers to the nearby Linz hospital. Karl promised he would be back within at most two hours; he just wanted to confirm Michael was alright.

Jim and the American GIs disapproved. Karl shouldn't be on his own that long. No, he wouldn't get approval to go to the hospital. They had more important things going on than wasting time at the nearby hospital looking for a patient whom they were not even sure was there. Michael could have easily been taken to any other hospital in the adjacent towns, because the Linzer Hospital had already been filled to capacity months ago.

"Don't you keep any types of records of the whereabouts of the Kranken?" Karl was irritated and even went to Marco to complain. Marco was also getting crankier as his time here went on: "Who has time to take detailed records of everyone? Our goal is to get the people here better. Let the historians sort out all the names and record keeping of what happened here." Seeing all the death, sickness and taking care of all the deathly ill while they were still dying daily was taking its toll.

"No" was the persistent response. They couldn't allow Karl to go the hospital to find his friend. He was, after all, still a POW. Karl then insisted that anyone who had to go to the hospital, maybe even one of the nurses could find out for him whether Michael Morgenthau was there. Marco vaguely assured Karl that he would see what he could do. It did not sound promising.

Michael was Karl's last connection to his *Heimat* (home) at this point. Lately Karl had dreamed of the scenario of them possibly even leaving here together: He had imagined how happy people on their suburban streets would be to see them both walk back home down their *Reichsstrasse.* But now Karl wondered when or if he would ever see home again. What would home look like? Would there be a home? Had it been bombed like many of the neighborhoods in Linz? He had witnessed the destruction in Linz and also had heard about all the other German cities having been bombed, the dead, the fires, the ruins and the homeless. They were now allowed to listen to the Allied radio stations and news of the bombings and devastation had traveled fast.

Daily, Karl and the young POWs continued to be shuttled to the concentration camp to do various chores, and after months of hard work the number of Kranken remaining was steadily shrinking. The bodies had been buried, and the Kranken who couldn't walk themselves or were in bad shape had been shuttled to hospitals or were at temporary lazarets the GIs had set up but the hospitals started to clear out. They had cured many, but also many of the prisoners still died even after the liberation — they had been too sick or too weak to recover from diseases like Typhus or tuberculosis. The number of 90,000 – 100,000 people murdered at Mauthausen did not account for the people who died after the concentration camp liberation, which was also in the thousands. But a good number recuperated, and some even walked out on their own. Even if not completely healed, they were eager to go home, often with nothing but the striped clothes on their bodies. [2]

Karl continued to puzzle over how many people had stayed quiet about the existence of this camp. *"Specifically, those in the surrounding areas must have known something and they stood by and just looked away? It was all just unfathomable. Granted, Germans living in distant villages or cities away from the concentration camps like my family could not have known or would not have believed any of this, even if they were told."*

General Eisenhower during his visit to Mauthausen had ordered soldiers to film the atrocities right after the liberations, and Marco, Jim, Sgt. Rotz and other GIs agreed they wanted the remaining buildings to be maintained for historical reasons and remain as a memory for all that had happened here. They wanted to make sure that this story here was presented for generations to come. The remaining KZ buildings had been cleaned up, any damaged furniture had been repaired, and at this point not much seemed to be left to be done.

---

[2] Karl later learned that the German population didn't really want to deal with or hear about the concentration camp prisoners. To empathize with them would have been an admission of guilt: guilty of knowing and not doing anything about it, or worse guilty of contributing to the atrocities. Not until decades later, when the new generations of Germans learned about the details of the atrocities, was sympathy developed.

Even the group of German teenage POWs at the internment camp was getting smaller. Karl was told that one group of the German POWs had been handed over to the Russians, and another group was handed over to the French. He was hearing that the Allied soldiers (Americans, Russians and French) would split up Germany. Linz was on the eastern side, and that possibly meant Russia would take over this area.

Karl continued to worry about being handed back over to the Russians. He wondered if the Red Cross could do something so that he and his *Kameraden* could be allowed to go home, instead of ending up with the Russians. He would even volunteer to stay and work for the Americans if that meant he wouldn't be handed over. After all he had been through enough, he couldn't imagine surviving the terror at a Russian POW camp.

One October morning while Karl was again getting ready for his daily shuttle to the concentration camp, before he could head out the door, Sgt. Rotz marched into their room and planted himself into the center of it with their bunk beds lining the walls and hollered: "You are getting out of here now, a train is taking you on your next journey!" Using the same tone he would use for any other order on any other day, Sgt. Rotz continued: "Get on that truck waiting outside. It will take you to the train station!"

Karl and his bunkmates could not believe what they were hearing. What did this mean? Take a train to where? Home? Russia? Where?

It was easy for them to get ready and "pack." They had nothing but the clothes on their backs. The date was October 11, 1945, a year after the SS had taken Karl from his home and over five months after he and Alois surrendered to the Americans on that dirt road near the railroad crossing.

"Where will the train take us? " Karl dared to ask, while still worried that they as some other captured teenage ex-SS will be handed over to the Russians.

Sgt. Rotz did not answer.

"Move! Schnell, schnell, get out of here!" he instead ordered.

The fact that he didn't respond worried Karl even more. Without a word about their quandary, they were all ordered to get on the same truck that had taken them to their daily KZ cleanup and carpentry tasks. Today it took them straight to the train station in Linz. As always, Sgt. Rotz was on the truck, but today he was there to assure they got on the train.

"That train on track 1 is the one you all get on!" he directed while pointing at it. Karl studied the train sitting on track 1waiting for them: The words written on the side of it were *Deutsche Reichsbahn* (German State Railway). It contained only cars for transporting animals: cattle cars.

Karl was sure that this was one of the many trains that had brought prisoners here to the camp. For a minute he wondered about the kind of men and women who were responsible for the transports of the KZ innocent lives and also the ones who actually drove the locomotive. They all contributed to the atrocities committed here in

Mauthausen. How did they justify transporting these prisoners? What about the men who shoveled the coal into the train's oven to keep it running? What about the many other railroad workers who maintained the tracks or took part in the prisoner transports? There were so many contributors, small cogs in the wheel, but they all contributed directly and indirectly. Everyone needed a job to support their families, and if one refused to do the work one was trained to do, no matter the consequences to other lives, they would have ended up unemployed with no other major skills, unable to feed their family. Worse, refusing an order, one could have ended up at the concentration camps with the rest of the prisoners. The options had been bleak.

Karl again wondered what his dad would have done, if he had been alive during this time. Would his name be added to the list of those who vehemently tried to fight the regime and ended up being killed? Or would he have faithfully done his job, regardless of the effect on thousands of other lives? The options seemed dismal: to sacrifice oneself to save lives or to stay quiet and live.

They were now filing onto the train: with armed Sgt. Rotz standing there, the young POWs didn't have much choice but to hop on. The train had no convenient steps to climb on, and without them, how did the kids and elderly people get off and on this train? How many fell and got injured?

Karl prayed the train did not take them to Russian territory, though the locomotive was facing east.

Once all had finally filed into one of the cattle cars, Sgt. Rotz slammed the big metal doors shut with a thunderous bang and with another loud thud they could hear the lock fall in place. Karl was sure this was the last he would ever see of Sgt. Rotz, and he would not miss him a bit. Sgt. Rotz had been a grumpy unpleasant soldier who despised the "Krauts" no matter what level their involvement in the war.

The closing of the cattle car door on the train ended Karl's chapter in American POW captivity. An unknown future awaited him.

With a rumble the train took off. Locked up, they all fell silent. If it wasn't for a few little rectangular windows, lining the top of the cabin, it would have been completely dark inside.

Overall the GIs had been good to Karl. They had saved him from the Russians, and a much worse fate would have awaited him with them. He would never forget the Russians killing the SS in that wide open field. In American captivity he was fed, clothed, and ultimately he had been able to contribute and help clean up the Mauthausen concentration camp. Karl considered it a privilege that he was allowed to help nourish back the sick and make them feel more comfortable. Mostly he was able to witness the outcome of the Nazi atrocities, and if he hadn't seen it for himself he could not have imagined the horror or was not sure he would have believed it, if anyone had just told him about it. He also became close friends with Frederick, Max and Wilfried, and he knew they would meet again someday. He found but lost Michael again. Fate had connected them here again in Mauthausen under the worst of circumstances. Karl continued to wonder about Michael's disappearance from the KZ and was still determined to find out what happened to him.

Karl and the other young ex-POWs took turns standing on the tip of their toes, pushing and shoving each other trying to get a better look out the tiny train windows.

The railroad workers couldn't have known what was happening to the prisoners at the camp, or could they? They had to have suspected something? The coal workers loading coal onto the train could have been prisoners themselves and were forced to do that work. Karl was trying to comprehend how so many could not have known about what was happening to the prisoners. *Could the locomotive driver have somehow saved them and taken the prisoners somewhere else to freedom? But to where?* Karl knew there had been plenty of spies everywhere who would have reported any missing train immediately. It would not have ended well for anyone involved.

"Where is this train taking us? If only I had a map!" Karl sat on the hard, straw covered cattle car, crammed in with his comrades. *"I wonder if our locomotive driver is the same who drove the prisoners. Or had the Americans arrested them and this driver is new?"* So many questions ran through his mind. *"What are the perpetrators doing now? Where are they now?"*

Even with the dim lighting, Karl noticed dark stains splattered on the wall of the train cab, and he knew it had to be dried up blood from the concentration camp prisoners. He wondered about how many prisoners had died even during the transport alone.

Karl needed to get his mind off all of this and he jumped up to join some of the others staring out the window. He now imagined breathing fresh air, and what he would give to smell the resin filled air in his Opa's carpentry. He so badly wanted to be home.

The boys continued to take turns in the train cab to stand tippy-toed, gawking outside. Whenever they could see a train station name they hollered it out, but while the train slowed down when it got close to some of the larger train stations and they got excited over and over again, the train never completely stopped. If they could only pry open the doors they could jump out.

The train continued to pass through numerous small train stations and small towns whose names they didn't recognize.

Sitting in their tiny crammed space they went around the cabin and each started talking about home. Surprised they learned that they were all from near the same areas surrounding Nuernberg, but since none of them had ever been to Linz in Austria before captivity they weren't familiar with this part of the country and they still could not determine with certainty where exactly they were heading. Though they were now starting to become more hopeful: they must have put them all on the same train, because they were from regions near to each other. Or was that just a coincidence? The train continued to rattle across the German country side: grassland, fields, hills, valleys, forests, cattle, some horses, but most unnerving to see were the buildings on fire and smoke rising high into the skies. The devastation was vast. Germany lay defeated. Everything passed by slowly, and everyone now looked on in shocked awe. Nobody said a word, each thinking their own thoughts of how Germany could have ended up like this, in rubble. The Germany that used to be known for its poets, engineers, musicians, and other great accomplishments was now known for starting two world wars. Karl thought, "*It must be the most hated nation in the world.*"

"We are going further east," one of the younger boys cried in fear and confusion, breaking the silence. He didn't look much older than 14. Was he right? Were they heading for Russia? It would take days to get there, though. They had no food, no water. If they made it there alive, they would never see home again, of that they were convinced.

A few then got together to try to pry open the doors again, squeezing their fingertips between the tiny metal space until they turned bloated and red, but the exit was safely locked from the outside. The KZ prisoners transported in here surely tried the same and none succeeded. The door and locks were unbreakable.

They sat back down again feeling defeated.

"Passau!" one of the boys glaring out the window screamed. It was finally a station they recognized: Passau! The boys were excited but the excitement quickly turned into astonishment. All Karl heard was *"Guck! Schau!* (Look there! And look here!)" Karl squeezed next to the boys and pressed his face against the corner of one of the windows to see what their bewilderment was about: he now clearly could see even more of the destruction: train tracks bombed, parts of the train-station building crumbled. The area was devastated. The lives they had known before the war would forever be gone.

"*How long would it take to rebuild all of this*," Karl thought aghast, as he also saw people, mostly women and old men, laboring away at removing the debris. It could be assumed that most of the younger men all had died in the war or were injured or captured and couldn't help. Rebuilding of Germany by the battle-worn and remaining Germans had begun, but the digging out from under the rubble would take years, of that Karl was sure.

Would they have to come to a complete stop because all the train tracks were impassable?

The train then slowed down to a crawl.

Karl continued to be amazed at what he was seeing. The destruction was immense. He already had seen the damage of the Allied bombings in Linz, during his daily transports from the POW internment camp to the KZ and in parts of the city, buildings there had been turned to rubble, brick over piled brick, and in some sections of the town streets had become impassable.

The train eventually moved on past Passau without coming to a complete stop and slowly sped up again and roared on. It would now have to pass through Nuernberg, of that they were sure. Karl dared to hope again:

"Hopefully the train stops in Nuernberg so we all can get off and finally go home." Karl thought out loud. "I can walk to my house from there."

"I'll get off anywhere it stops now. We can hitchhike home from anywhere near Passau," one of the boys mouthed.

"Right!" They all agreed, they were ready to just jump off, if only those doors would open. They were now in familiar territory.
"I can't take this much longer!"
"Me either!"
They had been on this train for over three hours now, they had not yet had any food or water that day.
"The war is over, they should let us out!" Karl chimed in. They all had enough and some were now banging their fists and kicking their feet hard against the door. As Karl was watching them, he suspected many of the concentration camp prisoners transported in this same train car tried the same, but as it had been for them, it was useless now. Nobody could hear them. The train was much too loud for the locomotive driver to hear anything. The driver had his orders and would follow them no matter what these boys were demanding. They were now really anxious for the train to reach Nuernberg, which they knew had to be the next big city. They would have to let them out then! After that the train tracks could only lead further toward the Russian demilitarized zone and then for sure they were going to end up in Russia captivity, if they didn't stop in Nuernberg, they thought.
After what seemed forever continued sitting helplessly mixed with standing eagerly looking out the window, one of the guys screamed: "Nuernberg! Nuernberg! Nuernberg!"
All of them now jumped up again and squeezed around the holes to the outside to catch a glimpse. It had been almost a year since Karl had last seen home. So much had changed for him. He had witnessed

things in his young life that nobody in any lifetime should have to see.

Would this train stop?

The brakes were squealing. The train was now slowing down.

Through the narrow windows they could see a Nuernberg that lay in ruins: destroyed railroad tracks, crumbled buildings, in the far distance the Nuernberg Cathedral's St. Lorenz church's tower stood, half-demolished. The Nuernberg old town was destroyed.

Here again old men, women and children were laboring away in the ruins removing the rubble. Broken cinder blocks would be put piece by piece onto a wheelbarrow and then dumped further down the road onto a pile of rubble.

He'd seen enough. Karl started banging so hard on the metal door, the skin on his knuckles cracked and they started to bleed. "They need to let us out!" He cried feeling helpless. He needed to get out of here and now. This was his only chance to finally be free. He needed to find out whether his family had survived the bombings. Was Hans home? Did he make it back? What about Hermann? Uncle Joseph? He missed them all so very much.

Then one started to scream "Let us out!" and one after the other they joined in and chanted "Let us out! Let us out!"

Finally, with a long loud screech the train came to a halt. The boys looked around in disbelief, then started cheering. Were they going to open the door? Would they let them go? "Open the door! Open the door!" they were now again hollering in unison.

“Shhhh!” one said putting his fingers in front of his lips, quieting everyone down. They could now hear some rattling outside their cattle car doors. Someone on the outside seemed to be working the lock.

With one loud pull the doors snapped open. Daylight poured in. Their eyes adjusted to seeing the locomotive driver standing there:

“Willkommen zu Hause! (Welcome home!)” He stood there in his coal-blackened uniform with his arms wide opened, with a yellow toothed, big smile. He knew this finally meant freedom for the boys. This was the end of the line for this train. The tracks were severely damaged, and the train couldn’t go any further. It was also the end of the line for these boys, and their time of witnessing one of the most gruesome chapters of history had come to an end.

As fast as they could, one after the other they jumped off the train. They were finally free.

Chapter 10

Today

Karl opens his eyes.
Slowly he looks around and sees an IV stuck in his arm and a thin hose leading to a drip. His chest is covered in probes that are connected to a heart monitor, and he now registers its rhythmic beeping.
He lifts up his head off the white hospital pillow and discovers Ellie lying in a cot next to him, still asleep. She had insisted on spending the night here with him.
He is in the American hospital in Virginia. They brought him here last night because of his heart issues, he recalls now, wide awake. Boy, what a good night's sleep he has had. The jet lag really did him in. Or was it the new medication? Probably both.
Dr. Schlesinger had insisted he spend the night here. And with the help of one of his health insurance representatives, Ellie got Karl on a Lufthansa flight back to Frankfurt, later today, leaving Dulles at 17:00. He will be flying first class, and an ambulance will be waiting for him at Frankfurt airport. Karl exhales deeply as he senses he is in good hands.
Dr. Schlesinger has now given clear and written instructions for Karl's health insurance and his German doctors: No, they can't ignore Karl's health needs any longer, even though he is 75. His heart medication needs to be adjusted and a stent needs to be placed as soon as possible. Dr. Schlesinger had told Ellie last night that she is a bit concerned about Karl's long overseas flight, but Karl insists he would not want to have surgery in a U.S. hospital and wants to be at home if there is any chance of dying. Dr. Schlesinger pressured

that he needed the surgery as soon as possible and that he is definitely traveling at his own risk. Since he insists on going, Karl will need to continue taking the new set of blood thinner medication she has prescribed.

Karl is somewhat concerned about his diagnosis, but at the same time he feels gratitude that a cardiologist with this doctor's credentials has taken the time to give him a more detailed check-up for once. "Socialized medicine!" he thinks and shakes his head. Ellie is so right, in the U.S. as long as you can pay for it, the doctors will take care of you. And in the case of Dr. Schlesinger's checkup, she didn't even charge the full amount. How can he ever thank her? Her efficient treatment during his one-day stay in the U.S. has turned out to be lifesaving.

On his flight back that evening, Karl thinks about his vivid dream about his WWII experiences. He is sure that he has now been rescued and saved a second time by the Americans. He now reminisces, as he often does, about his release off that train in Nuernberg that day. He will always remember the date of his own liberation: October 11, 1945. He and most of the boys exuberantly kissed the ground once they had one by one jumped off the train, then they each went their own way, one more eager than the other to get home.

Karl had stood on the side of the road and had stuck out his thumb to hitchhike home. Very few cars had passed by, very few roads were completely passable, but then a guy on a motorbike stopped and Karl had caught a ride on his back seat. Karl had held on as tightly as he could. He recalls enjoying the wind blowing across his bald head, and he couldn't remember ever feeling more free. But he was really anxious to get home. What would await him?

The driver had dropped him approximately 2 kilometers away from his home. Karl sprinted the rest.

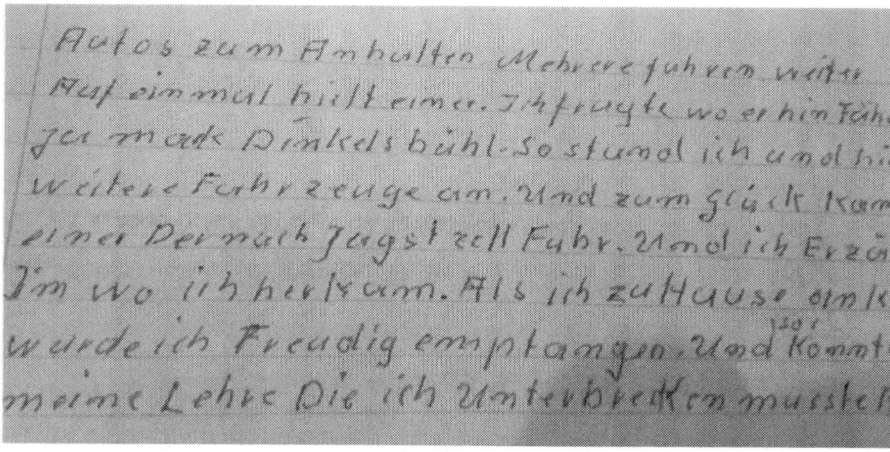

Autos zum Anhalten Mehrere fuhren weiter
Auf einmal hielt einer. Ich fragte wo er hin Fähr
Ja nach Dinkelsbühl-So stund ich und hie
weitere Fahrzeuge an. Und zum glück kam
einer Der nach Jagstzell Fuhr. Und ich Erzä
Im wo ich herkam. Als ich zu Hause ank
wurde ich Freudig empfangen. Und konnte
meine Lehre Die ich Unterbrecken musste

He had imagined his homecoming with much more fanfare, people out in the street welcoming him, maybe waving at him, but the roads were empty, and there was nobody on the way he could say hi to. Nobody was there to welcome him.

In the distance he saw his childhood home, Opa's house. It was still in one piece. The surrounding houses also stood untouched by bombs. He felt instant relief. He continued to run down the graveled road as fast as he could toward his home. Finally there, Karl ripped open the downstairs carpentry door and stormed in. *"They are still not locking the doors!"* Karl fleetingly thought. Opa was sitting in his usual chair, sanding, as if time had stood still for him.

Opa looked up and his eyes widened: “Karl!” He jerked up and the chair fell off his lap and as loud as his old, shaky voice allowed him, screamed in excitement. Karl ran over and hugged Opa.

“How are you?”

“Good, good and you? You look great!” Opa touched Karl’s face as if to inspect him to make sure he is still in one piece.

“Where is Mutter?” Karl was so excited and was already heading towards the steps as he asked the question. He now needed to see all his family members. Karl suspected the answer:

“Upstairs!”

Karl found Mutter in the kitchen. He had never hugged his mom that tight and long. Her face was instantly flooded with tears of joy.

“Where are Hermann? Hans?” Karl now knowing Opa and Mutter were fine needed to see his siblings.

“Hermann is his room!” Mutter answered, smiling.

Karl’s eyes widened. “So he was brought back the same night they took us?” He still couldn’t believe it.

“Yes!” Mutter nodded

Ferdinand had told the truth! Karl was incredibly relieved yet still surprised that Ferdinand had brought Hermann right back home, despite Albert’s orders. Throughout the war, there were numerous soldiers who remained humane and decent, after all. Karl was then sure, that Ferdinand was one of those soldiers.

Karl ran upstairs and found Hermann sitting in his wheelchair in his room by the window reading. Hermann’s red hair was cut short. The day after his brothers had been taken from their home by the SS, he had asked Mutter to cut it for him, in solidarity. He had kept it short ever since. He looked up at Karl, his eyes widened and his mouth was open, smiling the biggest grin. Karl smothered his brother with a bear hug.

"How have you been? I missed you so much!"

"Great!" Hermann was beyond excited to see his little brother finally back from war. They had worried so much about his whereabouts. Daily he, Mutter and Opa had prayed for his safe return.

"Have we heard from Hans?" Karl now asked Hermann. He needed all of his family to be reunited.

Hermann's big smile faded and he looked saddened at Mutter, who in the excitement of the reunion had rushed behind Karl up to Hermann's room. Karl followed Hermann's gaze and now looked at Mutter also.

Karl's heart sunk. He immediately knew the answer.

"We've received a letter from the *Abwehr.* Hans was shot and killed in Moscow."

"Moscow? How?"

"We don't know the details."

"Do we know when?"

"No."

Karl had bent over and let out the loudest groan as if someone had punched him really hard: "Noooooooooo!"

Mutter had rushed over and held him. She silently mourned with him. Karl had stood there crying in his Mutters arms for what it seems forever, when he slowly looked up at her again:

"Did we or will we get his body back?"
"No, he along with other German soldiers was buried in Moscow."
Karl now had confirmation he had lost his brother Hans in the war. In a way he always felt it – his gut had told him that he would never see Hans again that day the Russians separated them in that field in Linz. The exact circumstances of how he was killed or whether he really was killed or was kept in a camp until he died were never uncovered. They never found his grave in Moscow. They also never found out the whereabouts of Uncle Joseph. He had perished in the war, like so many. By the end of 1954, nine years after the war's end, the German military search service had identified 1,240,629 missing.[21]

After Hans and Karl had been taken by the SS that night, with only a few more days left to finish it, Opa and Mutter had readied the Major's desk for pick-up. Everybody, even Hermann, had worked many hours to finish it up. The Major had showered them with compliments, he couldn't have been happier with the outcome. He had paid them with plenty of food ration cards, which then were worth more to them than any Reichsmark, though supplies were even harder to come by as it got closer to Germany's defeat and capitulation. They never did find out who the desk and chair were for and never heard another thing from the Major, which was just as well for them.

Mutter and Opa also told Karl about the numerous air raid alarms during the last five months of the war. Everyone in the neighborhood used Opa's underground basement as an air raid shelter. One time, 50 people squeezed into that small space, people sitting on top of each other. Good thing the house was never hit, though a bomb detonated close by in the nearby woods where the kids had always played growing up. The bomb had left a huge crater in their neighboring forest. Nuernberg old town had been hit hard and the old city and the South train station lay in ruins. Not only were 5,000 people killed in the city alone but over 100,000 were left homeless. Karl had seen the destruction on his train ride in.

Mutter talked about the sand-mill factory only 10 kilometers away, which had been turned into a weapons factory the last 10 months of the war and was eventually also bombed. The owner and many factory workers were killed in the air raid. Mutter feared the factory owner and workers would not have been able to live with themselves after the war, since the factory's output directly contributed to prolonging the war and the killing of many. The factory owner and Mutter had been classmates during elementary school.

During the first four months of 1945, right before war's end, more bombs were dropped onto Nuernberg than between 1942 and 1944 combined. After July 20, 1944, more Nuernberg inhabitants died than in the previous war years.

Opa and Mutter went on to tell the story of the American parachutist who accidentally landed in front of Opa's house a few months back, completely off course. He had landed hard on their gravel road

leading up to their house and was badly injured. Mutter and Opa took care of him for weeks, and with the help of Dr. Magdalena, Sr., they nurtured the airman back to health. There were times they weren't sure he would make it. He eventually was strong enough to join one of his American troops again. Before the GI left, though, he insisted on shooting a deer for Mutter, Opa, and Hermann. It was his way of saying thanks to them for saving his life. The venison meat was the first taste of meat they had had in several months. It lasted weeks. Even though they still had the food ration cards, the butcher was often out of meat, rendering the food cards mostly useless. While they could pick blueberries, mushrooms and had some potatoes left in storage, neither Opa, Mutter nor Hermann would have been able to hunt for a deer or any other wild game.
Mutter would always talk about that reciprocating experience as another example of how so many of the soldiers remaining humane even during the war.

****

The pilot of the flight back to Frankfurt, Germany has radioed ahead regarding the heart patient on board in first class. As Karl's flight lands in Frankfurt, an ambulance awaits to take him to the nearby hospital. He is treated like a VIP: In the ambulance, he hands the written instructions from Dr. Schlesinger to the German medical technicians, to be handed to his doctors. Karl knows they will not ignore his health issues any longer. Because of that careful and considerate treatment and write-up from Dr. Schlesinger and the subsequent efficient treatment by the German doctors, Karl will go on to live another decade and a half. Karl will always claim that the Americans now have saved his life a second time.

Dr. Schlesinger visits her father that same evening she released Karl from the hospital. He is 76 and he has been a widower for nearly 10 years. Dr. Schlesinger likes to stop by to have dinner with her Dad once or twice a week.

"How are the therapy sessions going?" Dr. Schlesinger asked her Dad as he was setting the dinner table. Not until recently has he told her more about the details of his tragic experiences as a young man in the German concentration camp Mauthausen. She had known since she was a child that her grandparents had been killed there, and his concentration camp prisoner number tattoo was still very visible on his underarm, but while he generally has refused to talk about his captivity during the time she was growing up, he recently has opened up to her. He confirmed what they had always suspected about how badly her father had been tortured there: he had been beaten and nearly starved to death while forced to break rock on the Mauthausen quarry for over a year. That he survived there was a miracle. He still didn't really want to talk to his daughter about it too much more and at this point the topic is taboo.

Dr. Schlesinger had recommended that he see a therapist and talk it through there and he has reluctantly agreed.

“Fine!” he responds to her inquiry and then as usual he doesn’t want to talk more about it. Instead he now discusses the new BBQ chicken recipe he made today on his Foreman grill. He couldn’t wait for her to try it.

They are now sitting at the table in the dining room of his modest Georgetown townhouse, the remaining sunlight of the sunset streaming onto the dinner table through his large upstairs windows, while enjoying the healthy chicken dinner.

“Mmmhm, this is really good!” She confirms and he is content that this recipe is yet another success. He loves to cook and to please his only daughter who works so hard and he wants nothing more than to see her happy.

She then tells him of her office happenings that day as she does so often, since she really values her Dad’s input, a retired doctor himself. She discusses diagnosing this German man named Karl Elheusch with a heart condition, who was in Virginia visiting his daughter. She complains about Germany’s socialized medicine and how they there seemingly were ignoring Karl’s health needs, already having put him on the back burner in Germany at 75.

Dr. Schlesinger’s dad, Michael Morgenthau, replies stunned, “I used to know a guy named Karl Elheusch. He lived on my street growing up in Germany and he saved me at Mauthausen. I wonder if it is the same person. He is a really good guy! Where is he now?“

****The End****

Epilogue[vii]:

During World War II over 60 million people were killed, which was about 3% of the 1940 world population (est. 2.3 billion).[viii]

WWII casualties on the German side were high. The wartime military casualty figures compiled by German High Command, up until January 31, 1945, are often cited by military historians when covering individual campaigns in the war. Post war German estimates of military deaths range from approximately 4.3 to 5.3 million[ix] armed forces personnel. Civilian deaths during the war include air raid deaths, estimates of German civilians killed only by Allied bombing have ranged from around 350,000[x] to 635,000.[5][6][7]Civilian deaths, due to the flight and expulsion of Germans and the forced labor of Germans in the Soviet Union are disputed and range from 500,000[xi] to over 2.0 million[11][12][13][xii] In 2005 the German government Suchdienste (Search Service) put the total combined German military and civilian war dead at 7,375,800, including persons of German ancestry who lived outside of the borders of Germany and Austria.[14] This statistic does not include 200,000 German persons with mental and/or physical disabilities who were murdered in the Nazi euthanasia program.[15]

At the time of WWII, the United States had a large population of ethnic Germans. Among residents of the USA in 1940, more than 1.2 million persons had been born in Germany, 5 million had two native-German parents, and 6 million had one native-German parent. Many more had distant German ancestry. [xiii]

References:

[i] http://www.writing.upenn.edu/library/Parry-Milman_Historical-Medhod_1934.pdf
[ii] http://www.jmu.edu/stories/cohencenter/2014/09-2014/09-17-mcgann.shtml
[iii] https://savemetwice.com/2016/11/19/fake-news-propaganda-you-have-been-duped/
[iv] A few examples of Karl's writings, documenting his experiences during WWII, are placed throughout the book
[v] Richard Grunberger *A Social History of the Third Reich* (1971; London, 1987); 347
[vi] https://en.wikipedia.org/wiki/Mauthausen-Gusen_concentration_camp and "Mauthausen und Befreiung" Gerald Lamprecht
[vii] https://en.wikipedia.org/wiki/German_casualties_in_World_War_II#cite_note-7
[viii] https://www.census.gov/population/international/data/worldpop/table_history.php
[ix] Rüdiger Overmans, Deutsche militärische Verluste im Zweiten Weltkrieg. Oldenbourg 2000. ISBN 3-486-56531-1 page 228
[x] Rüdiger Overmans, Deutsche militärische Verluste im Zweiten Weltkrieg. Oldenbourg 2000. ISBN 3-486-56531-1 pp.147-48
[xi] Erich Hampe "Der Zivile Luftschutz im Zweiten Weltkrieg" pp.138-142 The figure of 500,000 includes 436,000 civilians, 39,000 foreign workers and prisoners of war and 25,000 police and military personnel.
[xii] Die deutschen *Vertreibungsverluste. Bevölkerungsbilanzen für die deutschen Vertreibungsgebiete 1939/50.* Herausgeber: Statistisches Bundesamt - Wiesbaden. Stuttgart: Verlag W. Kohlhammer, 1958
[xiii] https://en.wikipedia.org/wiki/Internment_of_German_Americans http://www.70-jahre-kriegsende.de/

Afterword:

After the war, my Dad Karl finished his carpentry apprenticeship and received the title of "Schreiner Meister" (master of carpentry). He proudly displayed the certificate in his carpentry shop.

He went on to produce many quality pieces of furniture and helped many people build their houses (roofs, doors, etc.) in his hometown.

He married my Mother and they remained married until she passed away, decades before his passing.

Throughout my childhood and growing up in Germany my Dad told us (his offspring) the stories presented in this book, describing his experiences during World War II, as a 16 year old in the war against his will.

Later in his life, I asked him to write his WWII stories down: I asked him many questions and he either wrote the answers down or I wrote the stories down as told by him. Throughout the book I included snippets of his writing, as examples, but there are many more pages.

Most all (approximately 95%) of the writing in this book is based on his true stories, but I also added some twists and turns, hence this writing is considered fiction based on a true story.

E. A. Dustin

65735475R00148

Made in the USA
Lexington, KY
22 July 2017